ROUTLEDGE LIBRARY EDITIONS:
WOMEN AND BUSINESS

I0130705

Volume 13

WOMEN, MICROENTERPRISE, AND THE POLITICS OF SELF-HELP

WOMEN, MICROENTERPRISE, AND THE POLITICS OF SELF-HELP

CHERYL RENE RODRIGUEZ

Routledge
Taylor & Francis Group

LONDON AND NEW YORK

First published in 1995 by Garland Publishing, Inc.

This edition first published in 2017
by Routledge
2 Park Square, Milton Park, Abingdon, Oxon OX14 4RN

and by Routledge
711 Third Avenue, New York, NY 10017

Routledge is an imprint of the Taylor & Francis Group, an informa business

British Library Cataloguing in Publication Data
A catalogue record for this book is available from the British Library

ISBN: 978-1-138-23710-0 (Set)
ISBN: 978-1-315-27106-4 (Set) (ebk)
ISBN: 978-1-138-24437-5 (Volume 13) (hbk)
ISBN: 978-1-138-28061-8 (Volume 13) (pbk)
ISBN: 978-1-315-27193-4 (Volume 13) (ebk)

Publisher's Note
The publisher has gone to great lengths to ensure the quality of this reprint but points out that some imperfections in the original copies may be apparent.

Disclaimer
The publisher has made every effort to trace copyright holders and would welcome correspondence from those they have been unable to trace.

WOMEN, MICROENTERPRISE, AND THE POLITICS OF SELF-HELP

CHERYL RENE RODRIGUEZ

GARLAND PUBLISHING, Inc.
New York & London / 1995

Library of Congress Cataloging-in-Publication Data

Rodriguez, Cheryl Rene, 1952–
  Women, microenterprise, and the politics of self-help / Cheryl Rene
Rodriguez.
    p.   cm. — (Garland studies in entrepreneurship)
  Includes bibliographical references and index.
  ISBN 0-8153-1969-X
  1. Small business—United States.   2. Small business—Government
policy—United States.   3. Self-employed—United States.   4. Poor
women—United States.   5. Entrepreneurship—United States.   I. Title.
II. Series.
HD2346.U5R63   1995
338.6'42'082—dc20   94-49558
                                                        CIP

To my parents, who dedicated most of their lives to me.

Contents

Preface

Theories on the amelioration or eradication of poverty abound. The American public is rich with ideas and commentaries on why the poor are poor, and on what can be done to relieve the federal government of its burgeoning social service responsibilities. Among the most recurring solutions to solving poverty are those that involve some aspect of self-help. Because the concept of self-help is associated with strength of character and an absence of laziness, we are sometimes inspired and often misled by Horatio Alger tales of economic triumph, and rags to riches success. Self-help, self-reliance, and self-sufficiency are indeed critical to an economically stable life. Yet, for economically disadvantaged women (America's poorest citizens), self-help is not as simple as grabbing sturdy boot straps or climbing illusive ladders. Creative ideas for self-sufficiency do not flower and flourish in environments that are void of resources. Often, the self-help process is initiated only when advocates speak for the voiceless poor, and encourage America's leaders to understand that women living in poverty need policies that are substantive and humanistic. What is a self-help initiative? How is the concept of self-help operationalized in a capitalist economy? How do advocates of self-help influence policy development? What role do self-help initiatives play in the lives of women welfare recipients? This book examines these questions by introducing the concept of microenterprise, exploring microenterprise's relevance to poor women, and describing the United States House of Representatives' attempts to formulate policy on microenterprise.

METHODOLOGICAL CONSIDERATIONS

This book is essentially a study of policy. Yet, it is markedly different from other policy studies in that it is both anthropological and feminist. While it is true that one can acquire knowledge of the policy process from a variety of social science domains, including political science, economics, and sociology, within these disciplines the fundamental stages of formal policy development are often generalized or presented as a linear process. An anthropological feminist account of policy formulation requires exploration of the intersection of gender and policy, analyses of interactions, professional relationships, continuities, and inconsistencies, as well as analyses of historical data. It requires observation, interpretation, and involvement in what Geertz calls the "sorting out of the structures of signification" (1973, 9). Inquiry of this nature requires examination from a humanistic perspective and, as such, lends itself to a qualitative research paradigm.

The epistemological basis for constructing a qualitative design for this research rested on the assumption that I could begin to understand the Congressional environment only by actively observing as many aspects of the Congress as possible, and by immersing myself in daily Congressional work. Often, data on policy analysis is based only on document analysis and interviews with policy specialists after the development of the policy. While analyses of the implications and potential impact of policy is of the highest import, descriptions of the policy process, from conceptualization to implementation, can illustrate policymakers' connectedness (or lack of such) with the realities of human life. An understanding of the true nature of this process can only be gleaned through participant observation.

Assuming the role of a participant observer in a contemporary, fast-paced, political environment, requires the same curiosity and heightened awareness that has served traditional anthropological inquiry since the 1800's. Indeed, participant observation has been referred to as the principal methodology of anthropologists (Barrett 1984, 28). Additionally, Crane and Angrosino (1974, 63) argue, "If any technique for field research can be said to be the most characteristic anthropological contribution to social and behavioral science, it is that of participant observation". Thus, by adopting the participant observer stance in this research, I utilized an enduring, multifaceted strategy to guide me in the study of the ever-changing phenomenon of policy. However, before establishing a presence as a researcher and forming relationships with Congressional staff members, I had to gain access to and acquire knowledge of the United States House of Representatives. Hence, it is necessary to discuss those factors and events which shaped the various roles I assumed during my research on Capitol Hill.

In August of 1990 I moved from Tampa, Florida to Washington, D.C. to participate in the Women's Research and Education Institute (WREI) Fellowship on Women and Public Policy. The WREI fellowship is a fifteen year old program which places graduate students in Congressional offices for one academic year. Among the goals of the program are to encourage effective participation by women in policy formulation, and increase awareness of national and international issues concerning women. I accepted this fellowship because of my academic interests and past political activism in issues which specifically affect women's lives.

Through WREI, I was offered entry into the United States House of Representatives as a Congressional Fellow. Many students apply for (and obtain) Congressional internships without the assistance and structure of a fellowship program. Like fellowships, internships allow participation in a Congressional office as temporary unpaid staff members. However, internship status on Capitol Hill is precarious. Interns are often relegated to copy machines, switchboards, and coffeemakers. Entry into Congress with the support and status of a highly respected fellowship program presumes a high level of education and professional skill on the part of the fellow. Theoretically, Congressional fellows assume responsibilities of professional staff members, including answering constituent mail, drafting legislation, consulting with governmental agencies, and attending Congressional briefings, meetings, seminars, and receptions.

The first role I assumed in Washington, D.C. was that of a WREI fellow. This required developing the confidence to negotiate and navigate my way around Washington, D.C. and Capitol Hill, interact with the seven other WREI fellows and the fellowship director, interview (during the first week of the fellowship) in several Congressional offices (the Select Committee on Hunger, the Select Committee on Children, Youth and Families, the office of Congresswoman Cardiss Collins, and the Congressional Caucus on Women's Issues) and determine my own placement in Congress. These were all intellectually and emotionally challenging events. However, the tasks of gaining entrance to Congress and becoming a part of the environment were made easier because of my role as a WREI fellow.

Prior to beginning the assignment with a Congressional office, I participated in WREI's three-week orientation program which included some of the basics on policy, politics, and procedure in the House of Representatives. The rigorous orientation schedule consisted of daily encounters with professionals who were in some way immersed in national policy work. There were parliamentarians from the Congressional Research Service and analysts from the Democratic Study Group, the American Psychological Association, and the American Political Science Association. There were staff members from Congressional entities such as the House Budget Committee, the Committee on Education and Labor, the Congressional Budget Office, and the Office of Technology Assessment. All of the speakers provided a wealth of very new information for the WREI fellows to process.

During my nine month tenure in Congress the WREI fellowship program served as a feminist framework for policy analysis and a guide to the formulation of questions for my research. Aside from our work in Congressional offices, each fellow was required to attend weekly WREI seminars with speakers who typically presented distinctly feminist or humanist perspectives on policy. Some of the discussion topics included: "Affirmative Action, Civil Rights and the Glass Ceiling for Corporate Women"; "Social Security and Income for Older Women"; "Women in the Military"; and "Women and Poverty". Additionally, there were meetings with members of Congress such as Democratic Representative Eleanor Holmes Norton, who described herself as "a feminist of the first order", and Republican Representative Connie Morella, who spoke of her support for a feminist agenda. There was also a meeting at the Supreme Court with Justice Sandra Day O'Connor, who, despite her conservative judicial background, spoke of the difficulties she faces as the only woman on the Supreme Court. All of these experiences reinforced my feminist views and helped me to shape the research questions that I, as a feminist anthropologist, would later ask.

During the orientation period and the weekly WREI seminars, I was able to learn about the Congressional environment, including the physical layout of the massive House Office Buildings. I also participated in the symbolic world of Congress by learning important Congressional terminology and procedures. Exposure to various political perspectives during the orientation and the seminars challenged the views on Congress which I had previously developed through reading newspapers, watching television, and through my work as a women's rights activist. I was also able to view Congress as a whole, which would later assist me in placing the Select Committee on Hunger in its proper perspective as a Congressional body. During the first week of orientation, I chose the Select Committee on Hunger as my Congressional placement. This decision was based on the rapport established with the staff during a one-hour interview. Also, I felt that this Committee would provide some particularly cogent insights on issues related to women and poverty.

The primary focus of my research was to actively observe the formulation of federal policy on microenterprise. However, before this could be done, a certain level of comfort and familiarity had to be established. This involved becoming a member of the Select Committee on Hunger staff, and assuming the responsibilities of a professional staff person. These responsibilities included interviewing and negotiating with the staff director for a nine-month staff position, arriving at the Committee staff office by 9:00 a.m. every weekday morning, claiming a desk, a chair, a computer (no small accomplishment), assuming a professional presence on the Committee's domestic task force, negotiating with the staff for the issues I would research, attending daily staff meetings and other required activities, attending social events with Select Committee staff members, and participating in the planning and drafting of legislation. This role as a researcher on the Select Committee was very similar to what Denzin (1989) refers to as the participant observer, who "makes her presence as an investigator known and attempts to form a series of relationships with the subjects such that they serve as both respondents and informants" (Denzin 1989, 163).

The secondary focus of this research was to observe training and support services at Business Owners Start-Up Services (BOSS), a microenterprise demonstration project in Baltimore, Maryland. After collecting some demographic data on microenterprise projects for the Select Committee on Hunger, I felt that it was important to experience the daily operation of such a project. Somewhat accidentally, I met the BOSS program director in a social setting. After listening to my research interests, she invited me to visit her program. My visit to BOSS involved participating in training classes strictly as an observer, interviewing six women who were students/participants in the program, and interviewing the program director. I later met with the program director again in a different setting for a formal interview. These observations and interviews provided insight on the administrative structure, operating procedures, and policies of a microenterprise training program. I also learned about the goals of some of the participants and the obstacles faced in attempting to reach these goals. My role as a researcher at BOSS was what Denzin (1989, 165) describes as the observer as participant, and involved two visits/interviews with respondents. My brief observations and interactions with the staff and students of BOSS did not permit an in-depth examination of the project. However, through BOSS, I was able to examine the concept of microenterprise outside of the federal policy setting.

Active participation with a professional staff such as that of the Select Committee on Hunger allows a researcher to grasp the critical factors that fuel decision-making and policy formulation. The researcher can also observe professional relationships between staff members, and the roles that staff members play in the work setting. Omvedt (1979) discusses this type of involved observation as a crucial method in the study of organizations. This methodology is also effective in gleaning information which would not necessarily be provided by a respondent in an interview.

While observation is a valid and valuable strategy for revealing the symbolic actions which compose human realities, there are also parallel strategies which enhance the researcher's quest for meaning. Denzin (1989) presents a "curious blending of methodological techniques" in his definition of participant observation as a "field strategy that simultaneously involves document analysis, interviewing of respondents and informants, participation and observation, and introspection" (Denzin 1989, 158). Steinmetz also contends that there are various tasks and strategies involved in participation observation, including "interviewing, filming, and the analysis of written records" (Steinmetz 1991, 420). Within the design of this research, document analysis and interviewing were chosen as significant enhancements to the active observation previously described. Document analysis included reading and interpreting Select Committee documents such as Select Committee Progress Reports from 1984 to 1990, Select Committee Issue Briefs, and Select Committee Hearing Reports. Additionally, correspondence to the Select Committee from various agencies, and news releases from the Committee, as well as news articles about the Select Committee were analyzed.

Interviewing included informal questioning and discussions with staff members during the early stages of the research. Later, as rapport and trust were established, formal interviews were held during office hours or after work. During the course of my time with the Select Committee on Hunger I interviewed one member of the international task force, two members of the domestic task force and one staff member who worked on both task forces. The primary informant (who provided a wealth of data on the history of the Select Committee as well as information on the policies, politics, and procedures of the Committee) was a person who had been with the Committee since its inception. Before working for the Select Committee, this informant had worked in other Congressional offices, and could therefore provide some seasoned insight on the culture of the United States House of Representatives.

ETHNOGRAPHY

The data-gathering strategies involved in this research permitted an interweaving of the subjective data with that which falls into the very tenuous realm of objective data. This combination of the subjective and objective speaks to the very core of anthropological epistemology and produces that which is known as ethnography. Despite its literary value, ethnography is interpretation, and interpretation is highly subjective. As Geertz points out, "anthropological writings are themselves interpretations, and second and third order ones to boot" (1973, 15). Nevertheless, the data on the Select Committee on Hunger is presented as a feminist ethnography, and serves at least two very necessary and significant functions in this study of policy formulation. First, feminist ethnography serves a descriptive function in that the inner workings of the House Select Committee on Hunger are described in detail. Thus, not only is the policy issue dealt with, but the daily work environments of the people who write the policies are described as critical aspects of the policy process. Secondly, the presentation of the data in the form of a feminist ethnography eschews the patriarchal notion of pure objectivity, and makes peace with the idea of subjectivity. In other words, through ethnography, the reader is made aware of the various roles played by the researcher in the research settings, and the pretense of complete, cold "objectivity" is never made. Thus, written observations, notes on information provided by informants, and analyses of policy, are blended to represent a combination of perspectives, including those of the researcher.

The subjective data, when combined with the so-called objective data (Committee documents, newspaper articles and other reports) present some reasonably sound ideas on the nature of policy formulation as this process occurred among the staff of the Select Committee on Hunger. Therefore, a major part of this book is concerned with understanding the Congressional environment that influenced policy formulation on microenterprise. However, this concern with policy does not diminish the very human elements of microenterprise including the significance of this concept for low income women. The most important goal of participating, observing, interviewing, and interpreting is to stimulate active discourse on the ways in which microenterprise policy could possibly support the ambitions of women with limited resources and opportunities. Through a careful and conscious interweaving of the subjective with the objective, some of the issues related to women's economic empowerment through microenterprise will be clarified.

Acknowledgments

From the conceptualization of the research project to the writing of the final word of this book, there were significant people in my life who listened, commiserated, advised and provided the necessary distractions for the completion of each chapter. It is to these people that I extend my humble gratitude and appreciation.

For her accessibility, suggestions on qualitative research, friendship and support throughout my research and writing, I thank Dr. Susan Greenbaum, chair of the Anthropology Department at the University of South Florida. I also thank my colleagues in the Africana Studies Program at the University of South Florida for their support. For her assistance and encouragement during my time in Washington, D.C., I thank Alison Dineen, former fellowship director of the Women's Research and Education Institute. A very special thank you to all of the WREI women of the 1990-91 fellowship year, especially Susan Messina, who listened patiently to countless drafts of my research ideas. I will always be indebted to the staff of the former Select Committee on Hunger, especially the members of the domestic task force, who answered questions, provided information and allowed me the freedom to explore the culture of the U.S. Congress on my own. I thank Cheryl Tates, Ray Bushara, and Patricia Johnson for participating in many hours of informal interviewing. I also thank the staff of Business Owners Start-Up Services in Baltimore Maryland, who allowed my quiet but noticeable intrusion. To Sharon Rogers, who assisted me with "insurmountable" computer problems, my gratitude. My daughters, Erica, Kiersten, Jessica and Erin Jensen, their father, Steve Jensen, my mother, Beatrice Rodriguez, my sister Debbie Rodriguez, my niece Joy Watkins, and my brother, Andrei Rodriguez, were as always, patient and loving during times when I may have been impatient and unlovable. Finally, to Dr. Daphne Thomas, who provided wisdom, laughter, love, food, a quiet working space, and a friendship that I will always cherish, my deepest affection.

Women,
Microenterprise,
and the Politics
of Self-Help

I

Welfare and Entrepreneurship: The Critical Intersection of Gender Class Economics and Policy

In a 1988 hearing before the Committee on Small Business, in the United States House of Representatives, Kathryn Keeley, of the Women's Economic Development Corporation (WEDCO), introduced some members of the 100th Congress to an uncommon notion. Ms. Keeley testified that a significant number of economically disadvantaged women have the desire, talent and motivation to create jobs in order to support themselves and their families. An expert on creative survival for women, Ms. Keeley developed WEDCO in St. Paul, Minnesota, in 1983. This nonprofit organization assists women, including those who are unemployed, or AFDC recipients, in achieving economic self- sufficiency through ownership of very small businesses (U.S. House 1988a, 205).

The hearing, entitled *"New Economic Realities: The Role of Women Entrepreneurs"*, was one of a series of six Congressional hearings held in April and May of 1988. The purpose of these hearings was to examine and document the discrimination that women entrepreneurs face in gaining access to credit and in obtaining Government contracting opportunities. The panelists consisted of successful women entrepreneurs who described the tremendous odds which they overcame in order to compete in the business world. Among the witnesses was Polly Bergen, noted performer and chair of the Polly Bergen Company, who testified on the validity and vitality of women-owned businesses. Describing her own success, Ms. Bergen recounted the story of her $3,000 investment in a cosmetic and fashion enterprise which led to a five million dollar business. Gillian Rudd, president of the National Association of Women Business Owners, testified on the economic impact women business owners have made on the national economy. Ms. Rudd appealed to the Small Business Committee and the Small Business Administration to take the lead in developing policies that would allow women's entrepreneurship to grow. Lillian Lincoln, owner of Centennial One, Inc., an eight million

3

dollar a year building maintenance company, spoke from the perspective of an African-American woman who started a business in 1976. Ms. Lincoln argued that, despite her high level of education and expertise in business development, customers, suppliers, and bankers were "slow to believe in a business plan" if it was submitted by an African-American woman (U.S. House 1988a, 12).

These testimonies by highly educated, economically privileged women, primarily spoke to the neglected but emerging relationship between gender and economic development policy. Indeed, women's roles as initiators, developers, and owners of businesses has been ignored. However, Ms. Keeley's testimony on WEDCO added another dimension to the discussion on women's needs for greater economic opportunities. Ms. Keeley brought attention to the critical interweaving of gender, class, economics, and policy by arguing that economically disadvantaged women, particularly those who are welfare recipients, are rarely able to pursue even modest dreams of business ownership. The stark realities of limited opportunities and restricted financial and technical resources, force many women to remain in very low wage jobs or connected to the welfare system.

What self-employment opportunities are there for poor and low-income women? Kathryn Keeley and other advocates for self-help initiatives argue that there could be and should be limitless opportunities for those seeking to take control of their own economic lives. These opportunities can be created through microenterprise, a term that became popular during President George Bush's Administration and is still used in President Clinton's economic development jargon. Quite simply, a microenterprise is a very small business. Such businesses are similar to, or evolve from, informal economic activities, and are often initiated with relatively minimal amounts of startup capital. These businesses are service oriented, labor intensive, and are usually operated by persons with limited financial means.

BARRIERS TO SELF-HELP

Among those persons who are most likely to operate microenterprises are low income women who are also recipients of Aid to Families with Dependent Children (AFDC), Food Stamps, the Special Supplemental Food Program for Women, Infants and Children (WIC), or other governmental assistance programs known as welfare.

Like other potential entrepreneurs, poor women generate ideas for businesses based on their talents, their family situations, or their dreams. However, welfare recipients face some extraordinary challenges in their attempts to begin microenterprises. One barrier is the difficulty in obtaining capital for business ventures. Access to even very small business loans is often impossible for low income women. Arguing that the transaction costs for these loans are high relative to the interests and fees, lending institutions see no profit in lending small amounts of money. Another barrier to business ownership for low-income women is the culture of banking which is founded on upper class, patriarchal, Social Darwinist beliefs in the value of competition. Low income women are invisible to bankers. Hoke (1990) gives several reasons for this invisibility. First, women microentrepreneurs have few, if any assets to use as collateral. Secondly, many women attempting to start businesses have no previous experience in the business world. Third, low income women, particularly public assistance recipients, usually have no significant credit history. Fourth, low income women entrepreneurs often lack sophisticated business or accounting practices.

The stigmatization of women welfare recipients by the banking community is only one of the many obstacles these potential microentrepreneurs face. There are many others, including a lack of support from welfare case managers and hindrances posed by family and friends. However, of all the encumbrances, the most formidable barriers to self-sufficiency are embedded within the welfare system itself. Welfare regulations specifically address self-employment, and include restrictions which are typically not imposed on middle class business owners. For example, in her efforts to develop a new business, a woman can lose welfare eligibility if she reaches certain assets and income limits. Even before a business has stabilized enough to provide adequate income for family support, the accumulation of working capital exceeding $1,000 can disqualify a family from receiving AFDC benefits. In most states, welfare recipients seeking entrepreneurship cannot separate business loans, or the value of capital equipment bought for a business, from personal assets. Further, welfare recipients cannot deduct repayment of loans as business expenses, nor can they deduct equipment depreciation (Feit and Das 1990, 3). The potential loss of Medicaid, Food Stamps, and subsidized child care are other severe barriers to business ownership for low income women. As with AFDC, income eligibility requirements for these programs restrict accumulation of assets over a certain dollar amount.

The 1988 hearing before the Committee on Small Business did not directly address issues related to the self-employment needs of public assistance recipients. Instead, the Congress proudly commending itself on acknowledging the success that a select group of women had achieved in the business world. Further, issues of class and ethnicity, and their impact on women business owners were only superficially addressed. However, in her final remarks, Ms. Keeley urged the Congress to consider the needs of economically disadvantaged women, as well as America's need for feasible and successful economic development models like WEDCO:

> The country is hungry for quick fix models to end poverty, create jobs and successful businesses and transform welfare recipients into tax payers. There are no quick fixes to solving poverty. Creating jobs and economic changes requires time as much as money. We must use a longer time frame and provide opportunities to the economically disadvantaged. They will then be better able to pursue their own ideas and develop their own opportunities (U.S. House 1988a, 30).

POLITICS AND SELF-HELP

Since 1988 both the Executive and Legislative branches of the United States government have made small steps toward addressing opportunities and choices for economically disadvantaged people. The Bush administration's response to America's outcry for answers to domestic poverty was a construct called the New Paradigm. Billed as an empowerment package, the New Paradigm featured allocations for "housing, education, enterprise zones, Indian affairs, small business and possible welfare reform" (Solomon 1991, 204).

The New Paradigm was full of lofty, promising ideals. It offered remedies to the housing, health care, education, and poverty crises facing America today. Yet, despite glossy rhetoric, some of which did receive bipartisan support, the New Paradigm was hollow political language from an administration struggling to piece together a domestic policy.

The Clinton Administration has also voiced its support for self-help initiatives, including programs that lend money to the poor for microenterprise development. As a candidate, Bill Clinton strongly advocated economic parity for people living in poverty, "I'll give people a chance to show that poor folks know how to borrow money, know how to pay it back, know how to make a living, and they have been deprived of that opportunity for too long." (Glastris 1993).

Despite campaign promises and good intentions, when self-help becomes a political issue, this very viable concept loses its vigor. For example, during the Bush Administration, empowerment packages were proposed at a time when the government was reluctant to spend money on any new social programs. This is also true for the Clinton Administration. In fact, most new initiatives are model programs or pilot projects which do not require significant governmental expenditures. Some economic policy analysts have expressed skepticism about the intentions and success of self-help programs that do not receive adequate financial support. In reference to President Bush's self-help proposals, one policy analyst commented, "Letting people help themselves would cost more than the White House is willing to spend" (Solomon 1991, 208).

Associated with the concept of self-help is the notion of empowerment, which has also become a part of both Democratic and Republican political jargon. In the 1960s and early 1970s, the concept of empowerment was based on liberal demands for social, political, and economic power to the disadvantaged and disenfranchised. Empowerment was synonymous with the political struggle for recognition of the rights of the poor. Activists involved in such movements as the Welfare Rights Movement, the Civil Rights Movement and the Unemployed Workers Movement understood that working-class and poor people must be a part of social change, not as victims but as actors. Thus, empowerment was dependent upon acknowledging the needs of people in communities, and facilitating community mobilization. In contrast, political leaders of the 1980s and 1990s view empowerment as a process that occurs on an individual level. For example, during the Bush Administration, the enlistment of the Small Business Administration for a project to support business ownership by the poor, was based on the assumption that the provision of credit alone, was the sole factor necessary for any entrepreneur's success. This assumption was based on knowledge of and reverence for the culture of the banking community, which is controlled by rich and powerful males. What was ignored was the fact that poor and low-income people, and in particular, poor women, are in need of a multitude of services (including technical assistance, legal assistance, child care, medical plans, and peer support) to ensure the success of a potential business. Moreover, this individualistic, competitive model also ignored those factors contributing to poor women's limited access to and control of the business environment. Those factors include low income women's lack of education about the business world, and their limited incomes which allow little contact with bankers.

In contrast to the rhetoric of ambitious politicians, grassroots advocates of microenterprise assistance programs have a perspective on this issue that is grounded in the realities of small business ownership by low-income women. Within the last five years, a growing number of advocates for microenterprise have persistently explored the concept of self-employment as one viable path toward self-sufficiency for Americans who live in poverty. Various groups affiliated with microenterprise have called for federal policies which would stimulate and support the growth of microenterprise initiatives across the nation. These groups also have sought changes in federal and state welfare regulations which would ease entry into microenterprises by public assistance recipients. A significant change being sought is one which would allow welfare recipients who are attempting to start microenterprises to continue to receive public assistance during the first year of developing their small businesses.

In attempting to affect radical but humanistic changes in welfare policy, persons involved in economic development through microenterprise have sought the cooperation of federal policymakers. Aside from testifying in Congressional hearings, directors and administrators of microenterprise assistance programs work with Congressional staff members to educate policymakers on microenterprise and to gain support for this economic development strategy. One Congressional body which was receptive to ideas posed by microenterprise advocates and thereby played an active role in investigating the economic needs of low-income women, was the Select Committee on Hunger. Before its elimination from the U. S. House of Representatives on March 31, 1993, this Committee was responsible for conducting comprehensive studies and reviews of the problems associated with global hunger and malnutrition, including the causes and effects of these problems. Originally authorized in 1984, the Select Committee on Hunger was involved with numerous issues related to health, hunger, and poverty. Some of those issues included: evaluation of food assistance programs; technology and development in economically disadvantaged nations; reduction of infant mortality; women in development; and measuring poverty in the United States. In 1991, the Select Committee developed comprehensive antihunger and antipoverty legislation in the form of an omnibus bill. One component of this bill, entitled "The Freedom

From Want Act", proposed to advance the concept of innovative self-help options for the poor in the form of individual development accounts for low income persons, and pilot projects for microenterprise initiatives. This may have been the first time that such an extensive self-help initiative was approached through the collaboration of a Congressional Committee and grassroots organizations. An account of that collaboration is one of the key aspects of this book.

THEORETICAL FRAMEWORK FOR ANALYSIS OF WOMEN'S MICROENTERPRISE INITIATIVES

Because nonprofit organizations such as the Women's Economic Development Corporation in Minnesota, the Women's Self-Employment Project in Chicago, Business Owners Start-up Services in Baltimore, and others across the nation have reported participation by a significant number of AFDC recipients, it is essential to ask how microenterprise can become a viable path to true economic independence for low income women who seek this option. Because policymakers can effect the kinds of support received by microenterprise assistance programs, it is important to consider the nature of the assumptions that inform policymakers' perceptions about women and poverty. It is also important to understand the politics of the policy formulation process and its relationship to the concept of self-help. Further, it is imperative to determine how emerging microenterprise policies address the particularly restrictive barriers to entrepreneurship which low income women face. These are the key issues addressed in this book.

The significance of addressing these questions lies in the revolutionary assumption that low-income women and indeed, public assistance recipients, do have a role in economic development. The potential of low-income women as creative contributors to economic development is a subject that is rarely explored. Rather, poor and low-income women are perceived as a mass of dependents contributing only to the expansion of the welfare state. This view of low income women is quite narrow and does not consider the multiple levels of oppression faced by this segment of America's citizenry.

Women, Microenterprise, and the Politics of Self-Help presents an anthropological and feminist analysis of microenterprise. This analysis addresses the critical interweaving of gender, class, economics, and policy, which must be considered in the development of any microenterprise support program. Thus, in this research, those entrepreneurial needs that are specific to low-income women were placed at the center of policy analysis. Additionally, this book views microenterprise as an economic strategy that has often been chosen by low-income women worldwide, despite cultural, historical, or governmental barriers.

The explication and exegesis of the key issues involved in this research require a theoretical orientation which explains the relationship of low income women to the state, the validity and significance of low income women's autonomous economic strategies, the role of the state in economic development policy, and assumptions about women's economic roles which inform policy formulation. Moreover, it is important to engage a theoretical orientation which suggests actions for resolving the problems involved.

Although feminist anthropologists have focused on women's political and economic relationships to the state, feminists such as MacKinnon (1983), have argued that feminism lacks a theory of the state. Moore (1988) contends that feminist anthropology is no exception to this rule. Thus, there is a need for theory which embodies both feminist and anthropological principles. The political economy school of anthropology allows analysis of low income women's relationship to the state by viewing the state and the capitalist world system as external forces which act upon classes or groups of people. Admittedly, there is an inherent weakness in the application of Marx's political economy theory to the economic strategies of low income women. Indeed, Marx was primarily directing his theories to "men and masculine circumstances" (Donovan 1987, 65). However, there are some important principles embedded within political economy which speak to contemporary feminist and anthropological thought.

Political economy incorporates cultural or symbolic issues into inquiry on the development of class or group identity, in the context of political or economic struggle (Ortner 1984). Accordingly, this book acknowledges the cultural integrity, the creativity, the capabilities, and the intelligence of low income women who are public assistance recipients, and describes one specific strategy which they may choose to employ for economic survival. Political economy also analyzes the larger systems of relations within which a group is embedded (Ortner 1984:142). Therefore, public assistance recipients and their families are viewed not only as a part of the welfare system, but also as a part of state and federal processes. Political economy also emphasizes the importance of history in anthropological inquiry. Ortner contends that this school of anthropology appears to be the most committed to a fully historical anthropology, and produces sustained and systematic work grounded in this commitment. Within this tradition, this research maintains an historical perspective on the development of federal policy on microenterprise.

Political economy is considered to be one of two distinct Marxist schools of anthropological theory. The other school of thought, structural Marxism, developed along with political economy in the late sixties and early seventies (Ortner 1984). In a discussion of the relationship between Marxism and anthropology, Clammer (1985) argues that the development of a Marxist anthropology radically confronted questions of colonialism, questions of the objects of anthropological inquiry, and questions of the theoretical foundations, and the moral purposes of the discipline itself. Clammer credits the political economy approach as one which allows anthropologists to see economic development as a process in which social, political, economic, and cultural factors are inevitably and inextricably mixed (Clammer 1985, 8). Further, political economy speaks to an action-oriented or practice approach to anthropology which assumes that the most crucial interactions are those which take place in asymmetrical or dominated relationships. Analysis of asymmetrical relations explains the larger system and highlights social asymmetry as the most significant dimension of both action and structure (Ortner 1984, 147). *Women, Microenterprise, and the Politics of Self-Help* assumes a humanistic perspective on the economic conditions of struggling entrepreneurs. Rather than attempting to categorize poor women or blame them for their poverty, this book addresses issues of power and oppression. Such issues have a direct impact on every aspect of these women's lives. Katz (1989) argues that mainstream discourse on poverty fails to include considerations of politics, power, and equality. This is true for liberal as well as conservative political thinkers. In response to this pervasive silence, this book is presented within the framework of "radical political economics" (Amott and Matthaei 1991, 4). With gender awareness at its core, this theoretical framework can address issues of power and dominance, and suggest strategies for the economic empowerment of economically disadvantaged women.

FOCUS AND SIGNIFICANCE OF RESEARCH

This book has a dual focus that contributes to the anthropological tradition of providing a holistic perspective of the research topic. First, there is a resolute focus on the formulation of microenterprise policy as this occurred in the House Select Committee on Hunger. However, looking at policy or the policymaking environment in isolation can render invisible those persons most affected by the policies. While it is essential that an applied anthropologist "work closely with public and private decision makers and special-interests groups in attempting to understand, measure, manage, and sometimes actually direct social and cultural change" (Chambers 1985), there is also the importance of "listening to others - to all the parties who engage in the negotiation of social legislation, including the 'target population' " (Sanday 1976, xviii). Also, defining microenterprise only as a policy issue limits the historical and anthropological value of the concept because we never see that this is a multidimensional concept that has been employed by women for centuries across cultures. Therefore, this book also focuses on understanding the political, economic, anthropological, and historical issues related to microenterprise, and the significance of these issues for low income women who are potential microentrepreneurs. With this in mind, Chapter Two is a literature review which takes an anthropological, historical, and political view of policy, microenterprise, and economic development for low income women. Although far from being totally inclusive, this literature review is extensive and does provide a multidisciplinary view of some of the complex issues that are particularly relevant to women's microenterprise development.

Chapter Three is a relatively detailed description of a microenterprise demonstration project, including the planning of the project, the administration and implementation of the project, and the participants who were enrolled in the project. Projects like the one described in this chapter were used as models by the Select Committee on Hunger for the development of legislation on microenterprise. Chapter Three stimulates discourse on a very new area of research. Thus far, no anthropological descriptions of a domestic microenterprise training program have been published. Nor has there been any anthropological research done on the role of microenterprise in state welfare reform. Therefore, Chapter Three opens the door to anthropological investigations of women, the state, and microenterprise assistance projects.

Chapter Four provides historical and ethnographic data on the Select Committee on Hunger, including some of the events leading up to the Select Committee's involvement with the issue of microenterprise. This is a critical chapter in that there may be no other scholarly studies of the House Select Committee on Hunger, a Congressional body whose nine year tenure ended on March 31, 1993.

At some point, historical data may be gathered and published on the accomplishments of this Committee. However, there will be no other ethnographic presentations by an anthropologist who worked as a staff member of the Select Committee on Hunger. Moreover, there are no anthropological analyses of the work of select committees. Therefore, this research can stimulate ideas on what can be done by an anthropologist in a Congressional setting.

Chapter Five is a description of the Select Committee's activities related to international and domestic microenterprise, including the development of "The Freedom From Want Act", an omnibus bill which supported microenterprise initiatives. Chapter Six provides a discussion and an analysis of the major themes and concepts of this book. Chapter Six also includes some recommendations for future anthropological research on microenterprise that can have a positive impact on policies, programs, and people.

Finally, *Women, Microenterprise, and the Politics of Self-Help* is an attempt to generate feminist thinking on the concept of microenterprise, as well as the productive roles that low-income women can play in the economic stabilization of their households and their communities. There are far too many unfounded myths and stereotypes about women and dependency. These need to be challenged. Gelpi, Hartsock, Novak, and Strober (1986) argue that perceptions of women as dependents results from the public/private dichotomy which connects men to the business world and women to the household:

> Women's lives are defined by their attachment to the private sphere, and in general, their low wages are not seen as an important public concern (Gelpi, Hartsock, Novak, and Strober 1986,4).

By describing Congressional policy activities related to women's microenterprise initiatives, this book challenges that dichotomy as well as the popular perception that women who are welfare recipients fail to seek economic independence. By explicating some entrepreneurship strategies of economically disadvantaged women, this book demystifies the concept of business ownership. By reviewing women's economic strategies across cultures, and illustrating how these activities precede domestic microenterprise initiatives, this book describes the shaping of an anthropological concept into a policy concept. By exploring the critical interweaving of gender, class, economics, and policy, *Women, Microenterprise, and the Politics of Self-Help* illustrates the use of microenterprise policy as a means of fighting women's poverty and contributing to women's economic empowerment.

II
Women, Microenterprise,
And Economic Empowerment:
A Global Perspective

The anthropological, historical, and sociopolitical literature on women's economic strategies provides evidence that women in all societies and classes facilitate economic continuity in numerous ways. Hence, women in all societies and classes (including low income women in America) need policies that will support and sustain their economic endeavors. Although anthropologists have documented and described women's economic activities, little has been done to analyze the policies that support or thwart these autonomous economic activities. One reason for this omission is that, historically, anthropologists have assumed a limited role in the policy process. Eddy and Partridge (1987) contend that there are three major reasons for applied anthropology's lack of vigor in contributing to public policy:

> ...the nature of policy formulation and implementation as a continually changing political process with which anthropologists have little familiarity, the fact that mainstream anthropology largely ignored contemporary social problems, and the limited use of empirical data of any type in many political decisions (Eddy and Partridge 1987, 381)

Anthropologists have described beliefs and traditions that influence the rules by which people of various cultures live. Research of this kind has demonstrated that policy is inextricably linked to even the most basic of human activities. However, as contemporary human issues become more complex and global, there is a need to understand the values and strategies involved in the formulation of national policies. Sanday (1976) proposes that through policy research, anthropology can serve the needs of both science and society, and that an ethnographic study of policy-related activities could lead to uncovering underlying assumptions and values motivating the cause of policy activity (Sanday 1976, xvi-xix). Chambers (1985) contends that the policy idea is intimately connected to applied anthropology because the work of anthropologists "can never afford to progress apart from the concerns of the rest of the world" (Chambers 1985, 37-38). Clammer (1985) argues that the future of anthropology lies in its engaging the issues of the contemporary capitalist state and of everyday life in the industrialized and industrializing world. Hence, it is clear that anthropologists can play a role in the study of policy formulation.

In discussing the anthropologist's connection to policy, Chambers (1985) argues that the anthropologist's sensitivity to cultural processes can be of great value in working with those who develop policies. Anthropologists should contribute applicable policy analyses that are theoretically sound. This can only be done by understanding the issues that are relevant to the people who will be most affected. With this in mind, the following discussion provides a foundation for the anthropological study of the policy formulation process on microenterprise by presenting research on women's economic development, women's economic contributions, entrepreneurship as an economic development strategy, and contemporary issues related to women and small scale business ventures.

RESEARCH ON WOMEN'S ECONOMIC ROLES

Although women's contributions to economic development are considerable, historically, these contributions have been unrecognized, minimized and unrewarded. Stevenson looks at data from the United Nations Decade for Women Conference and contends, "women do two thirds of the world's work, earn one tenth of the world's income, and own one one-hundredth of the world's property." (Stevenson 1988, 114). Gould and Lyman (1986) argue that women are a key constituency in the economic development process. Yet women's economic issues are generally relegated to a social service framework. Often, economic programs which focus on improving and protecting the health of the mainstream economy are aimed at economically advantaged males. Income maintenance and social service programs are aimed at women and minority groups, both of whom typically have little credibility within the mainstream economy (Gould and Lyman 1986, 4).

Joekes (1987) discusses the evolution of research on women's economic roles in societies, and looks at ways in which women's economic activities gradually have become central to national and international development issues. Early anthropological writings focused on women's traditional roles in domestic domains. Women's lives were examined within the boundaries of kinship, marriage, and local customs. Joekes contends that these narrowly focused studies were not intended to investigate women's participation in the economic milieu of various types of social organizations.

Evolving from anthropological studies were academic investigations from other social science domains. These studies on women's roles in economic relations ensued during the 1970s. Researchers began documenting and validating manifestations of a systematic subordination of women. A hierarchy in gender relations was also recognized. National and international development organizations turned their humanitarian concerns to "the relative status of the two sexes in law and social custom and on the need for women to be treated equitably with men" (Joekes 1987:3).

As the women's movement in many societies gathered strength, Western feminist scholars began to focus on the need to assert women's legal and political rights. In developing nations, feminist scholars were considering women's position within a cross-cultural perspective, linking topics such as decolonization, class struggle and ethnicity. Feminist scholars also identified the household as a microcosm of society, and not necessarily a haven against oppression for women. The household was characterized by "conflict among individuals at the same time as its existence is predicated on the gains they make from cooperating with one another" (Joekes 1987, 4).

A multidisciplinary approach to women's economic development emerged from these early anthropological and feminist perspectives. Joekes argues that economic growth was assumed to be the precursor of social, political, and cultural change for women. Perhaps strongly influenced by early anthropological studies, economic development research turned its primary interest to educational and employment opportunities for rural women. Joekes explains that within the multidisciplinary approach to the study of women's economic development there always has been a concern with women's work roles. Researchers interested in women and work have generally followed two approaches. One approach is a categorization of adults as either employed or unemployed, that is, either gainfully employed or seeking work. In various societies, women's concentration in informal sector activities led to their omission from statistical records. "The invisibility of women's work thus became a common complaint among some economists and policy makers" (Joekes 1987, 4).

The other approach to the study of women's economic behavior was an examination of the ways in which workers spend their time. Globally, women were shown to be working longer hours than men "across a spectrum of interrelated tasks that could not be sensibly divided into the conventional economic categories of 'productive' and nonproductive" (Joekes 1987, 5). Emerging from this approach to women's roles within economies was an understanding that women were primary providers of basic human needs. Nevertheless, strategies to improve women's economic lives continued to view women as beneficiaries of economic development rather than as participants. Relying on economic terminology, and paternalistic definitions of employment and work, development planners continued to omit women as an economic consideration except in social or welfare domains (Joekes 1987, 5).

WOMEN IN THE LABOR FORCE

Global analyses of women as wage earners indicate that women's contributions in the labor force are significant. In wealthy and poor nations, women's participation in the labor force increased dramatically between 1950 and 1985. Joekes reports that in 1950, 49% of adult women in developed countries and 37% of women in developing countries belonged to the labor force. By 1985, 57% of women in developed countries and 42% of women in developing countries were registered as part of the labor force. Joekes also notes that over the same time period, the numbers of men in the labor force fell in relation to the total male population, "so that there was a rather more pronounced rise in the proportional importance in the whole labor force than the increases in female participation rate implied" (Joekes 1985, 17).

Stevenson (1988, 114) reports that in 1985, 676 million women were recorded as part of the formal labor force. Millions of other women generate up to one third of the wealth in poor countries through their work in the informal sector. Despite this, much of the very necessary and very vital work done by women is not defined as gainful employment. Michon (1987) suggests that those duties which fall within the realm of women's work are those which are taken for granted: "on every continent, women farm millions of acres of land to feed people of their country; they produce up to 50% of the food stuffs available in the Third World. Each day, they process and prepare more feed people of their country; they produce up to 50% of the food stuffs available in the Third World. Each day, they process and prepare more food than the leading multinationals, supply villages with thousands, even millions, of tons of firewood, and carry billions of liters of water. Women meet the need for water, energy, food and primary goods of most of the earth's inhabitants" (Michon 1987, 30). Yet there is no economic value given to these tasks.

Despite the devaluation of women's economic contributions and work, Stevenson indicates that since 1950, the rise in female workers throughout the world has exceeded that of males by two to one (Stevenson 1988, 114). Gould and Lyman (1986) report that the number of women in the United States who support themselves and their families grew by more than 84% between 1970 and 1984 . Further, between 1970 and 1980, the percentage of female heads-of household with children under eighteen increased by 82%, for all families, and by 92% for African-American families (Gould and Lyman 1986, 6). Thus, women's work lives are in a tumultuous transition as more complex domestic and financial responsibilities are assumed. Nevertheless, women's salaries and wages are lower than those of men; women work disproportionately in low wage occupations; and women experience higher unemployment rates than men (Stevenson 1988, 114). More specifically, Amott and Matthaei (1991) report that although full-time work is twice as likely to lift a white single mother out of poverty than a Black single mother, in 1987, over 7% of full-time working white mothers were poor. These researchers also report that in 1988, Black women's full-time median income was less than 60% of white men's (Amott and Matthaei 1991, 189).

As crucial as a personal income is for most women, employment in the work force is not always the most effective path out of poverty. Phillips and Phillips (1983) suggest that women in the work force earn lower wages than men because of lower training and work experience, various forms of discrimination, and overcrowding-- "all of which have roots in the sexual division of labor in the family, the historical evolution of the market, and the laws of motion of the contemporary capitalist economy in which discrimination plays an important functional role in making the system work" (Phillips and Phillips 1983, 68-69). Job segregation and pay inequities restrict millions of women to low-paying jobs with very few opportunities for advancement (Gould and Lyman 1986). A consequence of women's low wages is seen in the growing number of women and children who live in poverty. Globally, poverty is a social and economic condition that primarily affects women and children (Stevenson 1988, 115).

The literature on women as workers indicates the necessity of including women in economic development policy and planning. However, in many cases, economic development policy for women has merely extended women's domestic roles rather than maximizing their economic potential (Stevenson 1988). Economic development has been defined as the process by which people, firms, and communities create new jobs and income by successfully adapting to changes in resource availability, technology, demography, and competition from other regions and abroad (Gould and Lyman 1986, 11). The goal of economic development for women should be to increase women's access to education and skill-training, credit, land, and the resources required to incorporate women into the economy (Stevenson 1988, 115). The success of economic development relies largely on nurturing and releasing the capacity for innovation and risk-taking. Thus, entrepreneurial skill-building and the creation of small businesses, can play a key role in the economic development process for women (Gould and Lyman 1986).

WOMEN AND THE CONCEPT OF ENTREPRENEURSHIP

Balkin (1989) reviews empirical analyses of independent economic activities in the United States and concludes that entrepreneurship has been increasing as part of the work force since 1970. Although this increase reflects a need and desire for independence in the work that one does, many business owners may not be considered entrepreneurial in the traditional or mainstream economic sense. Regardless of the terminology used to describe their ventures, there is greater participation by low income persons than the population in general (Balkin 1989, 45). Nevertheless, the role of women entrepreneurs (and particularly low income women entrepreneurs) in economic development has not been seriously acknowledged or explored by economic theorists. Stevenson argues that mainstream economic theorists focus solely on the achievement motivation of men entrepreneurs in societies (1988, 117). LaSota (1985) explains that although achievement is viewed as a key factor in entrepreneurial motivation, female achievement is seen almost exclusively in terms of supportive or dependent roles. Thus, it is often difficult for traditional thinkers to imagine women being in charge of their own economic futures through business ownership.

Balkin's (1989) exploration of some of the principal economic theories of entrepreneurship in society is indicative of the patriarchal models which influence many economists. In general, the classic economic theorists do not specifically address women and have not formulated theories that support women's independent economic ventures. Knight (1921) viewed the entrepreneur as one who receives pure profit for combining self-confidence, low risk aversion, and capital. Schumpeter (1934) viewed the entrepreneur as one who innovates by introducing a new product, introducing a new method of production, opening a new market, finding a new source of material, or creating a new type of business organization. Kirzner (1973) considered the entrepreneur to be one who looks for opportunities for profit when wrong prices exist in the market. Leibenstein (1978) considered entrepreneurship as a creative response to organizational inefficiency. Casson (1982) developed several entrepreneurial success principles which involved obtaining information, formulation of negotiating strategies, and the development of organizational skills. Regardless of the theorist, these theories perpetuate the mystique of entrepreneurship as a male dominated domain. This claim is made not necessarily because of the actual theories themselves, but because of the time periods in which they were created, and because women (as an economically oppressed group) are not specifically addressed. Also, many of the characteristics on which these theories are based (shrewdness, assertiveness, decision-making) have traditionally been viewed as inconsistent with what is though of as the female personality (LaSota 1985). Further, these theories do not address class or gender issues in entrepreneurship, nor do they address the significance of social networks, technical assistance, and availability of credit in business development.

Other social scientists such as anthropologists and sociologists have formulated theories of entrepreneurship that address ethnicity, gender, and culture. Mann (1989) acknowledges that although there are conflicting views on the determinants of entrepreneurship, some frequently cited characteristics are innovativeness, curiosity, hard work, orientation toward future, leadership, risk acceptance, selfishness and greed. Nevertheless, Mann points out that all of these characteristics have a variety of meanings across cultures. Thus, the meaning of entrepreneurship must be analyzed within specific cultural and gender domains. "Entrepreneurship is not something that is either present or absent, as a binary variable, but rather is a combination of factors. These are not to be measured on some absolute scale but can usually be understood only in local contexts" (Mann 1989,14). Friedman attempts to broaden the idea of entrepreneurship by including the concept of local context:

> There are entrepreneurs everywhere--in public housing complexes as well as Silicon Valley, on Indian reservations as well as MIT, in public agencies and Fortune 500 firms as well as new startups, in Youngstown as well as Austin, among the old and the very young as well as those in their late twenties and mid-thirties, among women and minorities as well as white males (Friedman 1987, 2).

WOMEN AND SELF-GENERATED ECONOMIC ACTIVITIES

Despite their absence from economic development theory and most entrepreneurial discussions, women's independent and self-generated economic activities have been documented by anthropologists. Research on women's economic activities in various cultures reveals a solid foundation of initiative, ingenuity, and entrepreneurship among women in many societies. Anthropologists have been particularly interested in peasant women's major roles in trade, petty commodity, and in the informal economy. For example, in a very general discussion of women's economic activities in peasant communities, Hammond and Jablow (1976) describe trade as one of the few occupations in which women may function outside of their domestic duties. Small scale markets serving the community are the settings for women's trade activities in household goods. Most traders provide garden produce, poultry, eggs, some handicrafts, and occasionally some imported items to sell or exchange (Hammond and Jablow 1976, 89).

Hammond and Jablow describe women's small market activities as peripheral to some local economies. Women of childbearing ages are primarily involved in traditional domestic roles and work only part-time in trading. However, in urbanized regions of West Africa, Southeast Asia and Latin America, these small local markets can be part of larger networks. As such, the necessity for commerce affords some women the opportunity to develop full-time trading businesses. Hammond and Jablow focus on the women of West Africa, whose trade activities have received a good deal of anthropological attention, and who often constitute as much as 80% of the total labor force in trade and commerce. Young girls learn the art and business of trade by observing trade activities of their mothers. At early ages, girls are given small sums of money on which to build a business. Initial enterprises for the girls may consist of selling a few cigarettes, matches, single lumps of sugar or small lengths of cloth. From this petty commerce, successful businesses have developed (Hammond and Jablow 1976, 91).

Hammond and Jablow also discuss the organized support through which West African women contribute to their economy: "The West African traders are organized into guilds which govern their commercial activities, controlling prices, supplies, relations with suppliers, customers, and political authorities, and discouraging competition from independent traders. The guilds also provide social services, such as mutual aid through insurance and provision for credit" (Hammond and Jablow 1976, 92). Successful West African women traders are described as highly-regarded and well-respected. These women are said to have uncommon initiative, ambition, and energy. Thus, "trade and entrepreneurship are ready-made outlets" for their energy (Hammond and Jablow 1976, 93).

Ehlers (1990) describes the women of San Pedro Sacatepequez, a highland Guatemalan town, who are the majority of the traditional labor force. The women are weavers, knitters, marketwomen, shopkeepers, and traders. Ehlers observes how family productive systems are greatly dependent upon the managerial efforts of women. However, while these women are expected to be skillful, independent workers, they are also expected to accept a secondary and subordinate status to men (Ehlers 1990, 2-3). The ingenuity, mobility, and entrepreneurship of the women of San Pedro Sacatepequez is also discussed. These women sell products which they produce themselves. However, their self-styled businesses offer limited economic rewards because these women have difficulty obtaining credit for expansion of their businesses. Another factor limiting these traders is that few women have access to lucrative external markets where export crops are traded. Both credit and the external trade markets are male domains. Many women traders invest all their earnings from trade into educating their children, particularly their daughters. Hence, trade, while not necessarily lucrative for the women, offers their children the possibility of a better future (Ehlers 1990, 85-108).

Research in economic anthropology has explored issues such as inland and overseas trade in various cultures, the interplay of sociocultural and economic factors on economies, historical continuity and local economies, and socioeconomic inequality. Although the economic anthropology literature on women's independent economic activities is not expansive, there has been some interest in the specific economic activities of women within various types of social organizations. For example, Barlow (1985) examines the role of women in intertribal trade among the Murik of Papua New Guinea. She argues that women's direct participation in trade is part of a general tendency in Murik society to proliferate social ties and extend their social networks. Barlow also observes that women's trade activities are consistent with other domains of Murik life in which women act independently in rituals, as well as in food production and distribution. Among the Murik, the work of women is essential for conducting every kind of trade (Barlow 1985, 120).

Dickerson-Putman (1988) addresses the important role of market income in modern peasant households of Papua New Guinea. She argues that previous research on Papua New Guinea markets failed to reveal the lucrative cash-earning opportunities for women in the markets. Accounts of women who attend the market for social rather than commercial reasons trivialized women's involvement in producer-seller markets. Dickerson-Putnam's participant observation and structured economic interviews revealed that women's market earnings in Upper Bena Bena are the second highest source of annual household income during the rainy season. Further, Dickerson-Putnam argues that the introduction of producer-seller markets was a significant development for the women of Upper Bena Bena because such trading offered the opportunity to earn and control cash independently (Dickerson-Putman 1988, 219-220).

Moore (1988), a feminist anthropologist interested in the changing lives of women across cultures, discusses the influences of capitalism upon women's work in peasant agrarian societies. When capitalism draws upon male wage labor, women's labor in peasant agriculture is intensified, but also, in order to meet personal and household expenses, women become involved in petty commodity production or petty commerce. Moore describes petty commodity activities as growing crops (for market as well as subsistence), brewing beer, making baskets or mats, or selling processed foods. Moore indicates that, although men and women both participate in petty commodity or informal economic activities, women's involvement is of a particular kind. Arizpe's (1977) study of stratification of informal activities by class among women in Mexico is an illustration of Moore's point. Although middle class and poor Mexican women participate in the informal economy, middle class women usually have husbands, and therefore, work at home. The middle class women in Arizpe's study performed such services as tutoring and sewing (activities which would be done free of charge for family members). In contrast to middle class women, poor Mexican women work in the streets or in homes of other women. Moore argues that, in the case of the Mexican women (in Arizpe's study) these independent economic activities provide supplementary incomes for middle-class women and basic survival incomes for poor women (Moore 1988). From her exploration of various anthropological studies of women's independent economic activities, Moore concludes that, because women are often forced to enter economic activities in a different way than men, the processes of class formation are gender specific.

Bunster and Chaney (1985) observe migrant women who work as street vendors and domestic servants in urban Lima, Peru. Sellers and servants work as a part of the informal sector, but can become part of the unregulated, uncounted and "shadowy world of the casual labor market" (Bunster and Chaney 1985, 5). These women workers represent the largest groups of employed women. Yet Bunster and Chaney argue that little is known about their occupations because most studies of migrants are concerned exclusively with males. Supporting economic development for poor women in developing countries, Bunster and Chaney argue that the most important way to assure women's participation in development is to support and enhance the productive activities in which women are already engaged (Bunster and Chaney 1985).

Anthropological studies provide rich cultural documentation and theoretical analyses of women's abilities to identify economic need and respond to this need by developing independent, income-generating enterprises. Historical data also makes a considerable contribution to the story of female enterprise. Stevenson (1988) notes that, despite restrictions from the Church and State, women have engaged in entrepreneurial activities over many centuries. Stevenson cites one example from thirteenth century European history in which a group of unmarried women began supporting themselves by weaving, lacemaking, embroidery, and nursing. These women set up industries, and formed corporations. However, their assertiveness was challenged by the Church and local commerce. The State acted against these women by seizing their property and burning at the stake those women who continued to defy the Church. The story illustrates the western world's legacy of intolerance for female autonomy.

Stevenson cites another example of women's attempts at economic autonomy in an historical account of sixteenth century England. During this time, women engaged in a variety of self-generated economic activities such as spinning, brewing, and supplying horses, jousting equipment, wheels, and armor to the king. Under strong pressure from the Church, a fixed role, defining women in terms of marriage, eventually emerged. Women who acted independently were subject to serious sanctions, and their businesses were ruined (Stevenson 1988,117).

These historical examples illustrate women's struggles against the patriarchal powers of the Church and State. Contemporary female entrepreneurship also faces formidable social, political, and bureaucratic barriers. However, women's autonomous economic ventures are increasing. Women worldwide look to independent business ownership as an alternative to low wages or welfare. Stevenson notes that in 1980, only 5% of employed women in the United States owned and operated businesses, compared with 12% of employed men (Stevenson 1988, 119). LaSota reports that in the United States, women-owned businesses represent the fastest-growing segment of the small business sector. In 1983, 27% of all sole proprietorships were woman-operated, and in 1985 the Small Business Administration estimated that there were three million woman-owned businesses (LaSota 1985, 5).

Although extensive socioeconomic data on women business owners is very limited, some researchers (Hoke 1990; Gellatly 1990; Gould and Lyman 1987) indicate that a considerable number of women welfare recipients are developing businesses. Poor women are particularly invisible to researchers and policy makers interested in economic activity. Thus, the literature on entrepreneurship by poor women in America, and particularly women who are welfare recipients, is grossly inadequate. Few researchers have investigated the number of welfare recipients who engage in independent economic activities, who attempt to become self-sufficient through business ownership, or the strategies used by poor women to overcome barriers to business ownership. Most of the data on this population comes from those entrepreneurial assistance programs which specifically target low income persons. Therefore, it is important to understand the general organizational structure, the goals, and the history of entrepreneurial assistance programs in the United States.

ENTREPRENEURIAL ASSISTANCE PROGRAMS IN THE U.S.: A BRIEF SURVEY

Although a very common form of assistance into self-employment is through informal networks of family or friends (Balkin 1989,136), a growing number of local private nonprofit agencies and community organizations are providing support for the concept of self-sufficiency through business ownership. Entrepreneurial support agencies are developing in response to an increase in the self-employment rate which has consistently risen since 1970 (Becker 1984). Self-employment has increased due to rising income tax rates, increasing unemployment (Long 1982), the growth of a service-oriented economy, an increase in contract work to smaller firms, and an increase in the number of women entering the labor force (Balkin 1986).

Many entrepreneurial support agencies provide technical assistance, networking, and referral services specifically for low income persons interested in starting businesses. Phillips (1990) indicates that there is much geographical and organizational diversity among microenterprise projects. Some projects, such as Micro Industry Rural Credit Organization in Arizona, focus on a particular business sector. Other projects, such as Women's Ventures in St. Paul, Minnesota, are gender specific. Still other projects may be associated with Small Business Development Centers, university programs, Displaced Homemaker Programs, or credit unions (Phillips 1990).

Balkin (1989) examines fifty entrepreneurial training programs for low income persons in the United States and classifies these programs by the following three dimensions: target population (which can be a specific low income group such as women, or low income persons in general); type of training (which can be industry linked or general self-employment training); and program focus (some programs emphasize a business plan while others do not). The most numerous microenterprise programs for low income persons are programs providing general self-employment training, programs targeting specific groups, and programs which focus on developing a business plan (Balkin 1989, 114-116).

Phillips (1990) discusses some of the national nonprofit organizations in the United States which work on microenterprise development in urban and rural areas. In 1990 there were approximately one hundred organizations, such as the Charles Stewart

Mott Foundation in Michigan, and the Ford Foundation in New York, which provided grants for local or national microenterprise projects, as well as for evaluation and policy development. In addition to these efforts, the Ms. Foundation in New York organized several national foundations including Mott and Ford, Levi Strauss, and others to fund local organizations involved in microenterprise for low income women (Phillips 1990).

Another type of self-employment project, the Unemployment Insurance Self-Employment Demonstration, was initiated by the U.S. Department of Labor. As part of a plan to accelerate reemployment of unemployment insurance recipients, the project allows the recipients to use their benefits as start-up capital for small business development. The federal Omnibus Budget Reconciliation Act of 1987 permitted the establishment of a demonstration program utilizing unemployment trust funds to assist unemployed persons in pursuing self-employment. Pilot projects began in Washington State in September of 1989, and Massachusetts in May of 1990. These projects are currently testing the effectiveness of three forms of allowances for unemployment insurance recipients: one-time lump sum payments, a series of payments over time, or some combination of the two forms. In addition to the allowances, the programs provide basic self-employment training. The models for this program are the Enterprise Allowance Scheme in Britain and the Chomeur Createurs in France. Although there is no mandatory training component, both of these European programs allow eligible unemployed persons to use their benefits to create businesses (Wandner and Messenger 1990).

A HISTORY OF U.S. MICROENTERPRISE PROGRAMS

The United States government's involvement with self-employment for low income persons began with President Johnson's Great Society programs. In the early 1960's, job training and small business assistance programs became popular economic development strategies. Perhaps the intense focus on poverty was an astute political move to diffuse some of the angry demands of the Civil Rights and Welfare Rights movements. The administration's zest for "an economic drive against poverty" (Piven and Cloward 1979, 268) was operationalized in the development of the Model Cities Program and the Office of Economic Opportunity. By organizing local and regional community development corporations, these federal programs attempted to foster initiatives that would employ the poor (Mott Foundation 1989). The passage of the 1964 Economic Opportunity Act authorized the Equal Opportunity Loan Program. Administered through the Small Business Administration, the program offered relatively large unsecured loans (seldom below 25,000), but did not include adequate entrepreneurial training components. Enormous default rates brought these programs to an unsuccessful end (Mott Foundation 1989).

Self-employment, specifically for African-Americans, was an issue in Richard Nixon's 1968 presidential campaign. Black Capitalism was a political movement which referred to the economic development strategy of stimulating business formation in black communities. During Nixon's administration, programs such as the Local Business Development Organization (BDO), Minority Enterprise Small Business Investment Companies (MESBIC), Business Resource Centers (BRC), and Office of Minority Business Enterprise sprang up to assist black enterprise (Balkin 1989, 82). However, Balkin argues that Black Capitalism as a government policy was merely a continuation of policies initiated during the Johnson administration involving loans from the Small Business Administration and minority set-asides for government contracts. Support for unskilled, low income entrepreneurs was quite inadequate (Balkin 1989, 81).

In the 1970s assistance programs for small, economically disadvantaged businesses were administered through Community Development Block Grants (CDBG) or through the Economic Development Administration. However, the primary focus of these projects was on bringing enterprises into depressed communities, rather than encouraging self-employment of community residents. Later in the 1970s and into the early 1980s, approximately twenty-one programs under the Comprehensive Employment and Training Act (CETA) provided entrepreneurial training for low income persons. Although the programs did reinforce the concept of business ownership for CETA-eligible clients, these small programs were costly, and its recipients were those who would more than likely be successful with or without the support. Criticized for selecting only the "cream of the crop", CETA was discontinued in 1982 and replaced by the Job training Partnership Act (JTPA), which presently funds self-employment training programs (Balkin 1990, 49).

HISTORICAL MODELS FOR MICROENTERPRISE PROGRAMS

Contemporary projects which assist economically disadvantaged persons in achieving self-sufficiency through microenterprise bear some similarities to immigrant/ethnic group social networks or mutual aid societies of the nineteenth century. These historical networks, independently organized by such diverse ethnic groups as African-Americans, Asians, Euro-Americans, Afro-Cubans, and West Indians, promoted economic autonomy by providing business networks, apprentice opportunities, loan funds, and moral support to its members (Balkin 1990, 47). Greenbaum (1991) emphasizes the economic aspects of mutual aid societies which have been ignored by economists, historians, and anthropologists. While these societies strongly supported ethnic solidarity and cultural nationalism, they also generated significant capital through dues and activity funds. With the capital surpluses, the mutual aid societies provided medical benefits, or loans for houses, education, or small business development (Greenbaum 1991, 3). A contemporary version of the mutual aid society is the rotating credit association. Velez-Ibanez (1983) observes the rotating credit associations of Mexicans in Mexico and the southwestern United States. Like other cultural inventions, the activities of the rotating credit associations are "repeated, regularized, and sometimes linked to ritual " (Velez-Ibanez 1983, 3). These associations function as savings, lending, or borrowing organizations in which the members have access to relatively large amounts of money, while at the same time, the members participate in the rotation of these resources. Yet, more importantly, these associations represent an attempt by poor or working class Mexicans to reduce the uncertainty of their economic lives (Velez-Ibanez 1983).

Although there are some distinctive differences between mutual aid societies, rotating credit associations, and microenterprise programs, many contemporary entrepreneurial assistance programs are based on models of group support rather than the rugged individualist model on which the American capitalist system is based. The philosophy and ideology of lending support to entrepreneurs with limited resources, is apparent in today's microenterprise training projects. As such, entrepreneurial assistance programs reflect an extension of the concept of kinship and group support. These concepts have remained essential in human survival and are crucial to the development of microenterprise.

DEFINING MICROENTERPRISE

Despite a growing number of microenterprise programs in Third World countries, Europe and the United States, a clear, uniformly accepted definition of the concept has not been established. Because of differences in political ideologies as well as economic structures, American policymakers often attempt to make marked distinctions between microenterprise activities in developing nations and those microenterprises in the Western world. In a report submitted to the United States Senate Small Business Committee by Coastal Enterprises, Inc., microenterprises in developing countries are described as informal, family-based, tiny business operations involving small amounts of loan money (Phillips 1990, 3). Berger, focusing on microenterprise projects in Latin America, defines microenterprise as an economic segment of the informal sector, its informality being distinctly characterized by such factors as internal organization, relations with the outside world and process of production (Berger 1987, 5-7). Mann, Grindle, and Shipton (1989) present a cross-cultural perspective on microenterprise, and express concern about attempts to connect microenterprise to any particular segment of the economy. However, the definition presented by these researchers strongly implies some of the elements of informality that have been recognized by other researchers: "...'micro' will mean those with no more than about ten permanent members, and no more than U.S.$10,000 fixed assets. The number of persons may include family members of a single nuclear or extended family. Generally, a small or microenterprise is one whose disappearance would make no appreciable difference to the national or international market in which it operates" (Mann, Grindle, and Shipton 1989, 10).

In contrast to the focus on informality of microenterprise in developing countries, the report from Coastal Enterprises defines microenterprise ventures in the United States as formal, incorporated or unincorporated businesses employing less than nine person (Phillips 1990, 3). In a report on the significance of microenterprise to Southern regions of the United States, Hoke describes microenterprises in terms of their low visibility, the family-based nature of these operations, their service sector orientation, and the lack of formal connections to the business community (Hoke 1990, 1-2).

What emerges from these perspectives on microenterprise is the notion that there are some basic aspects of very small scale economic activity which defy attempts at circumscription, specification, and clarification. One barrier presents itself in the forms of regional, cultural, political, economic, and circumstantial variations between entrepreneurs. Clearly, microenterprises operating in rural communities are significantly distinctive from those operated in an urban autocratic military state.

Another barrier to concisely defining microenterprise is the culture-specific meanings of such terms as work, enterprise, business and self-employment. For example, there are at least three African interpretations of the term "self-employed", including Zambian use, which emphasizes autonomy; Ghanaian use, which specifies working for two or more persons; and Swazi use, which emphasizes being paid by the job (Mann, Grindle, and Shipton 1989, 27). Hoke mentions regional perceptions of self-employment in the United States, including small business operators in southern regions who do not define their endeavors as actual businesses. Other barriers to defining microenterprise include variations in types of businesses as well as the changing structure of any given business activity.

Despite differences between microenterprise activities in the United States and those in less wealthy nations, there are significant similarities which should not be ignored. Acknowledgment of these similarities contributes to the formulation of sound economic development models. In fact, some researchers (Hoke 1990; Balkin 1989) argue that many important lessons can be learned from Third World models of self-employment for the poor. Thus, the most productive way of viewing microenterprise is in terms of the process represented by microenterprise activities. In both wealthy and poor nations, microenterprise represents a way of operating a business. Because of economic restrictions, microenterprise represents those strategies through which low income entrepreneurs initiate and operate businesses. In general, microenterprises can operate as very small components of commercial networks, distributing goods and providing services. As in large scale businesses, there is variation in the number of persons employed and in the duties of employees. However, microenterprises generally employ between one and ten persons (Hoke 1990; Phillips 1990; Mann, Grindle, and Shipton 1989).

Microenterprises require very small amounts of start-up capital (ranging from $50.00 to $5,000), and often evolve out of economic necessity in areas where there are limited formal job opportunities (Hoke 1990; Phillips 1990). In general, microenterprises are concentrated   microenterprises are low visibility, the close connection between business and family, and the inherent flexibility of these ventures. These descriptors are not unlike those features which characterize activities of the informal sector. Because of these similarities, it is important to understand the concept of the informal sector and the relationship of the informal sector to women and microenterprise.

MICROENTERPRISE AND INFORMALITY

The concept of the informal sector has captured the interest of diverse groups, including anthropologists, development specialists, economists, Marxist structuralists, and others concerned with the alleviation of poverty. The term, "informal sector" was first used by the British anthropologist Kieth Hart in his descriptions of the economic activities of the urban poor in Ghana (Peattie 1987; Mezzera 1989). Hart assigned this term to a range of self-generated activities in the subsistence economy of an exploited majority of city dwellers. Since Hart's 1973 paper, various perspectives on the informal economy have broadened the concept beyond its original categorical boundaries.

Mezzera (1989) challenges the misconceptions which were a part of the original definition of the informal sector. One misconception is that the informal sector is an illegal economy associated with evasion of taxes and other state regulations. Mezzera notes that formal sector firms have also been known to evade taxes. Yet, more importantly, informal businesses are not established to avoid taxes, but to survive. Another misconception is that the informal sector results from distortions in the labor market resulting from mistaken economic policies. According to this belief, policies such as the imposition of minimum wage or the actions of labor unions cause wages to rise above their equilibrium level, creating a surplus labor supply. Theoretically, if the minimum wage were eliminated and trade unions were less powerful, there would be a reduction in surplus labor and in informal economic activities. Mezzera responds that even in countries where the minimum wage has been eliminated and the power of trade unions has been destroyed, the informal economy continues to flourish (Mezzera 1989, 46).

Mezzera also challenges the notion of the street vendor as the only manifestation of the informal sector. Although street vendors are a highly visible part of the informal economy, Mezzera contends that they do not account for all of it. Mezzera identifies another commonly held view which defines the informal sector as all self-employed workers, unremunerated workers, and domestic servants. This definition is challenged by Mezzera's argument that the informal sector is not a set of people, but a set of enterprises or productive units, encompassing a range of economic activities (Mezzera 1989, 46).

Finally, Mezzera challenges dualistic economic models of the formal and informal sectors established by economists in the 1950s and early 1960s. Although there are various dimensions of these dualistic conceptualizations, these models stress the contrast between two sets of economic activities. The formal sector is presented as relatively profitable and privileged; the informal sector is viewed as relatively disadvantaged (Peattie 1987, 852). These dualist economic models contrast modern structures which appear to have no relationship to what is considered traditional structures. Mezzera contends that indeed, many economic relationships exist between the two sectors, "The sectors buy from and sell to one another in the same way that the center and peripheral countries of the world buy and sell; the informal sector 'exports' to and 'imports' from the modern sector" (Mezzera 1989, 47).

Portes (1989) contends that the informal economy should be understood as a process rather than as an object. Although a majority of persons engaging in informal economic activities are poor, these processes cross socioeconomic structures. Portes explains that the informal economy should not be perceived as a euphemism for poverty, nor should it be thought of as a set of survival activities engaged in by marginal persons. Instead, the informal economy should be seen as a process of income-generation which is "unregulated by the institutions of society, in a legal and social environment in which similar activities are regulated" (Portes 1989, 12).

While informal sector work is characterized as unregulated, those microenterprise ventures which are connected to entrepreneurial assistance programs, are subject to state regulation. However, it is not uncommon for a participant in an entrepreneurial assistance program to have vast experience in established "unregulated", "unorganized" and therefore, "invisible" businesses. Connection to a microenterprise assistance program can enhance business skills, provide business networks, and offer avenues to credit assistance. As such, these invisible ventures become connected to conventional business structures and achieve some element of visibility. However, in organization, size, and processes microenterprises operated by low income persons continue to resemble informal businesses.

INFORMALITY, MICROENTERPRISE, AND WOMEN'S WORK

Informality and microenterprise are concepts which complement a significant segment of women's economic endeavors. Berger (1989) denotes five characteristics shared by women's work, microenterprise, and informality. These are internal organization, relations with the outside world, variability of business activity, limitations on technology, and lack of separation of consumption and production. The first characteristic is internal organization. Employment roles within informal sector activities, microenterprise and some work done by women are necessarily flexible. That is, a self-employed worker in a very small enterprise can act as worker, manager, and owner of her business. Another characteristic is relations with the outside world. Relationships of informal sector workers with suppliers, clients, and the state are often less defined than those relationships in which formal workers participate. Formal contracts, flexible hours of operation, and irregular business hours can characterize informal businesses, microenterprises and the work in which women are typically engaged (Berger 1989)

Variability of business activity also connects informal work with microenterprise and women's work. The existence of combinations of different activities, the simultaneity of activities, and the frequent changes in activities are all characteristics of these kinds of work. A fourth characteristic connecting informality and microenterprise with women's work is the limitations on technology. The process of production is hampered by the microentrepreneurs' inability to purchase expensive technology. Limited access to working capital often forces these business owners to cease production when necessary raw materials run short.

The fifth characteristic linking the informal sector with women and microenterprise is the lack of separation of consumption and production. Berger explains that economic theorists view consumption and production as different domains. Thus, policies and programs aimed at improving production and income generally ignore consumption (except in terms of demand for additional products). In very small business ventures with limited resources, "business expenditures, income, assets and labor are inextricably linked to those of the household" (Berger 1989, 7). Moreover, reliance on living quarters, vehicles, and other personal assets, often keeps very small and informal businesses somewhat solvent. Women's participation in informal and microenterprise ventures is particularly affected by the lack of separation of consumption and production. "For women in the informal sector, an added dimension is the simultaneous use of time for domestic and business purposes; nowhere is this clearer than in the case of child care" (Berger 1989, 7).

MICROENTERPRISE ASSISTANCE PROJECTS FOR WOMEN

The interconnection between informality, microenterprise, and women's work forms the basis of some of the most successful women's microenterprise projects in Third World countries and in the United States. In economically disadvantaged countries, there are various organizations which administer microenterprise projects. At least four of these organizations have made more than 10,000 microenterprise loans annually (Hoke 1990, 6). Research data on evaluations of these programs indicates that the most successful projects emphasize the provision of credit rather than extensive training and feasibility analysis. Hoke (1990) cites a 1985 study conducted by ACCION International for the Agency for International Development, which contended that the most effective international microenterprise programs include the following characteristics: good leadership; seriousness about client commitment; a concerned and dedicated staff; a focus that shapes projects to meet clients' needs; a community-based mechanism for participant selection; the ability to reach a reasonable number of clients; flexibility in meeting client's needs; concern with effective administration; avoidance of paternalistic attitudes; and avoidance of excessive formality. These characteristics should be considered in the development of domestic microenterprise assistance projects (Hoke 1990, 6).

Women In Development Programs

The Women in Development (WID) literature provides examples of microenterprise projects which include the characteristics mentioned by Hoke. For example, Reichmann (1989) describes the quality and extent of women's participation in microenterprise projects in the Dominican Republic and Peru. In Lima, Peru, the Progreso program was created to strengthen the numerous businesses of the informal sector. Progreso's goals also include increasing income levels and creating new employment for the poor. Informal lending practices combined with elements of formal lending contribute to the client's level of comfort with the program. Progreso's elimination of collateral requirements, reduction of paperwork, frequent repayment option for vendors, and regular meetings at the Progreso office for program participants, all contribute to an element of informality and accessibility. The extension of a line of credit encourages the participants to develop long-range goals for their businesses as well as plans for increasing productivity (Reichmann 1989, 142).

Eligible microentrepreneurs are required to form solidarity groups of five or eight members in order to borrow from Progreso. Each member of the group must be willing to guarantee other member's loans. Progreso utilizes the group loan mechanism for several reasons. First, extending credit to groups is more cost-effective than credit extended to individuals. Second, the groups become promotional vehicles for the program. Third, technical assistance can be provided for the group in one session rather than individually. Fourth, group facilitators communicate with group members about regular attendance at Progreso meetings or training sessions (Reichmann 1989, 139).

Progreso attempts to reach 80% of women and 20% of men in the informal sector. The emphasis on women is critical because women represent the majority of market vendors. Further, women have the least amount of access to credit, women are viewed as very responsible with credit, and Progreso assumes that women use business gains to support families. Reichmann reports that despite Progreso's efforts to target women, women's participation is only 52%. However, those women vendors who do participate in Progreso operate businesses which are faring almost as well as men's businesses in terms of income increases and generation of new jobs. Reichmann also reports that women gain confidence by participating in Progreso. Further, Progreso's staff reports that women's repayment of credit is more responsible than the male participants (Reichmann 1989, 143).

Reichmann also describes women's participation in the Association for the Development of Microenterprises, Inc. (ADEMI). Founded in 1983, ADEMI assists informal sector businesses in Santo Domingo, Dominican Republic. Upon its inception, ADEMI included a solidarity group lending component and a lending scheme for individual microentrepreneurs. However, in 1987 ADEMI phased out its solidarity group program. Individual business owners must demonstrate the ability to invest more capital in equipment, machinery or services in order to qualify for a loan. The loan approval process is relatively simple, requiring an application which is processed within a few days. Upon receipt of the loan check, the microentrepreneur is accompanied to the bank by an ADEMI staff person, who assists in using the bank's services and (opening up) a savings account. All participants are encouraged to deposit portions of the loan check in savings accounts, since savings are required for future loans (Reichmann 1989, 146).

        The level of women's participation in ADEMI primarily reflects women's overall level of self-employment in manufacturing and services in the informal Dominican economy. In 1986, 22% of ADEMI's total participant population was composed of women microproducers and vendors. ADEMI's women microentrepreneurs are generally older than the male participants. Also, the women microproducers have an average of one more year of business experience and one more employee than the businessmen. Nevertheless, women's businesses earn slightly less per month than men's (Reichmann 1989, 148).

        The Women in Development Program of Partnership for Productivity Service Foundation Kenya (PfP/K), is an international nongovernmental agency which provides special training and credit assistance through a group loan program. Participants in this program are women who operate small agriculturally based enterprises. Massive male migration to urban areas of Kenya have left many Kenyan women with the responsibilities of managing households, raising children and providing for families through subsistence farming. Women in rural Kenya perform 60% of the agricultural labor, 50% of the animal husbandry, 60% of the marketing, 90% of the domestic water and firewood collecting, and 80% of self-help projects (Gould and Lyman 1987, 71).

        Despite their highly visible participation in farming, Kenyan women traditionally have been denied access to the necessary training and credit for developing their agricultural activities beyond the subsistence level. Most of the agricultural training programs have focused on male farmers; most credit institutions generally do not lend money to women. In an effort to remedy these historical biases, PfP/K expanded its microenterprise development program in 1984 to include a training and credit component for women (Gould and Lyman 1987, 71)

        Building on Kenyan women's informal social and savings groups, PfP/K assists groups of women in obtaining credit. Traditionally, rural Kenyan women organize in groups and make weekly contributions to a group savings fund which can meet the consumption needs of individual members. PfP/K works within the framework of the group. In order to qualify for assistance a group must have a bank account, be legally registered, be willing to save regularly, and have taken on some type of joint economic project (such as a community water tank or animal husbandry project). PfP/K provides initial capitalization for a revolving loan fund controlled by certain group members (RLF Committee). The RLF committee is responsible for recapitalizing the loan fund within a thirty-month period with money obtained from borrowers' required savings contributions and interest payments on loans. The RLF committee also makes small, non-collateralized loans to individual women at commercial interest rates. While 70% of the loans support agricultural ventures, 30% support women's small-scale commercial endeavors (Gould and Lyman 1987, 73).

Through the assistance of a PfP/K field officer, the women's social groups establish policies and develop administrative mechanisms for their group's loan program. Local loan fund committee members also have exposure to national development issues at annual conferences. Field officers also monitor loan fund progress and provide assistance to individual microentrepreneurs. In 1987, there were sixty RLF committees operated by women's social groups. According to the researchers, "By the end of the thirty-month period, most groups are economically self-reliant, and group members have acquired the ability to administer the fund, make responsible loan decisions, and provide business counseling to one another" (Gould and Lyman 1987, 73-74).

Some of the innovative approaches to fighting women's poverty in South Asia include the development of the Self-Employed Women's Association (SEWA) and the SEWA Bank in India. Based on the Gandhian principle of 'Antodaya' (which means starting with the poorest), SEWA originated as a response to the inability of conventional trade unions to deal with those issues related to poor women in the informal sector. SEWA's emergence was also influenced by the trade union movement as well as the women's movement in India (Wignaraja 1990).

SEWA's origin was the women's group of the Textile Labor Association (TLA) in Ahmedabad, India. TLA, a conventional trade union, had a women's group. However, the interests and needs of poorer and lower caste women who worked in the textile factories on a piece-rate basis, were not supported. Further, TLA was primarily interested in formal employer-employee relations. SEWA began with the assumption that linkage to the formal credit system could make poor women independent of money lenders. "This assumption was gradually changed with experience and SEWA also established its own bank" (Wignaraja 1990, 74).

Issues raised during the growth of the women's movement in India clarified the fact that the struggle of poor women involved an interrelated set of problems including social, political, and economic aspects of life. With this realization SEWA provided a comprehensive organizational framework for the poorest women. Once SEWA was organized, the establishment of a bank validated the concept of poor women's right to economic independence:

> The trade union of poor women in the informal sector and the bank became mutually reinforcing, in both the struggle against injustice of various kinds as well as for sustainable development through the building of alternative co-operative economic and social structures (Wignaraja 1990, 75).

SEWA has approximately 21,000 members organized into small groups according to their economic activities. Each group elects a leader; the leaders of the groups form the association's representative board. From the representative board, an executive committee is elected to manage the association. Initially, SEWA acted as an intermediary between the poor women's groups and the nationalized banking system by guaranteeing loans. Although the banks granted loans at four percent, the complicated and time-consuming bank procedures as well as the attitudes of male bank staff, contributed to the problems of poor women working in the informal sector. Credit alone could not solve many of the women's problems (Wignaraja 1990).

In 1974 the SEWA Bank began operations with a total capital of US $5,500. By 1975 the bank had 9,000 depositors and a total capital of US $33,000. The repayment rate on the SEWA Bank loans is nearly 90 percent. By eliminating the constraints of the formal banking system, the bank institutes an innovative advocacy approach to the lending process. For example, photographs replace signatures for identification purposes. New norms that relate to the reality of poor women's lives are used to determine credit worthiness (Wignaraja 1990, 76-77). Through the Self-Employed Women's Association and the SEWA Bank, women receive organized support and credit assistance for their microenterprise ventures. Poor women are freed from the exploitation of moneylenders and are able to generate income to support themselves and their families (Wignaraja 1990).

By far the most highly publicized and well-known development project dealing with poor people's economic autonomy is the Grameen Bank in Bangladesh. Although its focus has not been specifically women, some researchers (Hoke 1990; Wignaraja 1990) indicate that women's participation has been particularly high due to their traditional lack of access to credit and employment opportunities. The bank began in 1976 as a research project to determine the affects of credit assistance to the poor in an impoverished village near Chittagong University. Dr. Muhammad Yunus, an economist who obtained a doctorate in the United States, initially attempted to encourage local banks to lend money to the landless poor for business development. The difficulty of working with the traditional banking system led Dr. Yunus to create a bank to serve poor people in the immediate area of his university. The lending scheme expanded to other villages, and in 1979 became a formal project. In 1982, the Grameen Bank was recognized by the government of Bangladesh as a specialized bank. In 1986 sixty percent of the capitalization of the bank came from the government and outside agencies and the remainder from customers (Balkin 1989, 98).

The Grameen Bank is organized in individual units which cover an area of 15 to 20 villages. A field manager and bank workers administer bank policies. Persons owning a half acre of cultivable land or less are eligible for loans. However, potential borrowers must form groups of five people. In keeping with local Islamic tradition, group members must be of the same sex. However, bank rules also require group members to have similar business interests. During a month long probationary period, the potential borrowing group becomes familiar with the Grameen Bank policies. The groups also determine if the members are conforming to bank rules and make certain each member can write his or her signature. A chairperson and secretary are elected during the group's weekly meetings. During weekly center meetings, loan proposals are discussed, loan disbursements are made, and payments are collected (Balkin 1989, 98).

Upon completion of the probationary period, two group members are permitted to apply for individual small loans for any economic venture. When these first loans are repaid, larger loans may be obtained. Most loans are repaid within a year through weekly installments of two percent of the principal plus interest. Loans to other group members are contingent upon the repayment behavior of the first borrowers. If, after two months, the first borrowers maintain responsible repayment behavior, other group members become eligible for loans. The entire group is responsible for the repayment of any loan defaulted by a member (Balkin 1989, 99).

The Grameen Bank is one component of a political, social and economic struggle involving the mobilization of poor women and men in order to move out of poverty. It is also "an example of an alternative banking system for the poor, primarily women. It has become a public sector organization functioning with new norms, financial discipline and sound management at all levels" (Wignaraja 1990, 40). Following Bangladesh's independence struggle of 1971, the Grameen Bank began in a single village and currently encompasses 7,502 villages, providing loans for over 339,000 persons, 81 percent of whom are poor women (Wignaraja 1990, 41). In its attempts to mobilize the poor and move them toward capital accumulation and asset creation, the Grameen Bank has five major objectives. The first is to extend banking facilities to the poorest men and women in the community. The second is to eliminate exploitation by moneylenders. The third goal is to create opportunities for self-employment for the unemployed and underemployed. The fourth goal is to provide an organizational structure which the poor can understand and in which they can participate fully, thereby increasing their economic, social and political strength through mutual support. The fifth goal is to expand poor people's ability to invest credit and increase income (Wignaraja 1990, 41-42).

The Grameen Bank has also been viewed as a vehicle which supports women's microenterprise ventures through an emphasis on financial assistance to the very poorest persons. Balkin (1989) and Hoke (1990) also argue for the adaptation of certain Grameen Bank principles to microenterprise programs in the United States. There are some concepts of the Grameen Bank which could be translated to Western principles. First, the idea that collateral should not be paramount in acquiring loans. Instead, peer group pressure and access to further credit could be motivation for repayment. Second, borrowers could initially receive very small loans. After establishing credibility, larger loans could be provided. Third, loans should be scaled to the U.S. economy, taking into account U. S. incomes and the average start-up capital for microenterprises (Balkin 1989, 104).

There are some difficulties in attempting to adapt every aspect of the Grameen Bank model to the United States. Balkin (1989) argues that in Bangladesh, the poor have many opportunities for participation in the informal economy. These informal microenterprises may pay better than alternative wage labor. However, the primary barrier to microenterprise development in Bangladesh has been the limited availability and access to credit by the poor. In the United States, poor citizens, have access to some social service resources, and minimum wage jobs. According to Balkin, these resources often pay better than self-employment. The "safety nets" of welfare or low paying jobs are unavailable in Bangladesh (Balkin 1989). Thus, the economic situations of the two countries are quite different. "Abundant self-employment opportunities are a constraint in the United States. To parallel the simple types of unregulated self-employment activities in which people participate in Bangladesh, one needs to look at the informal sector of the U.S. economy" (Balkin 1989, 104-105).

Peer Lending for Women in the United States

At least five microenterprise assistance programs in the United States have adapted the Grameen Bank's peer group model (Hoke 1990). This model is a novel approach to microenterprise assistance in the U.S., and its feasibility has yet to be demonstrated. However, program administrators have found that the peer group concept is gaining acceptance and support in their communities (Hoke 1990, 9).

The Women's Self-Employment Project (WSEP) is an example of a microenterprise peer lending programs in the United States. Located in Chicago, Illinois, WSEP is a non-profit organization, funded by private foundations, government agencies, individual contributions and fees. WSEP assists low and moderate income women in achieving self-sufficiency through self-employment. The services provided by WSEP include orientation sessions, self-employment workshops, twelve weekly entrepreneurial training sessions, individual consultations, technical assistance and business loans. The primary goal of the program is to help women in the realization and use of their creative business skills and to apply these skills toward microenterprise (Gellatly 1990).

WSEP fills a major gap among economic development strategies for low income women by acknowledging these women's marketable skills and validating the use of these skills for economic survival. WSEP's Executive Director contends that the organization assists those who are typically ignored in the U.S. economic development sphere:

The potential for low-income individuals -
particularly women- in economic development is far
from fully tapped. How can we advocate increasing
economic development and ignore the talent and
skills of an entire group of people based on the fact
that they happen to have less money than others?
That is what low-income means. Less money, not
less creativity, perseverance, common sense, or
ability to think (Gellatly 1990, 1).

WSEP focuses on individual empowerment while also
addressing women's roles as family members and community
members. Thus, the benefits of microenterprise for low income women
can affect individuals, families and communities both economically
and socially:

There is the potential for increasing individual
wealth, and increasing the economy of the low
income neighborhood in which the new entrepreneur
lives and works. Children of these entrepreneurs
become exposed to ownership and business.
Exposure to role models then becomes a factor in
breaking cycles of welfare dependency within
families. People in low income communities,
particularly children, become aware that other
options and opportunities exist for them (Gellatly
1990, 1).

The Women's Self-Employment Project was conceived in the
spring of 1985 when a group of individuals representing various
women's and community organizations convened to discuss issues
related to low income women. The impetus for the meeting was the
realization that 78 percent of the nation's poor were women and
children. In Chicago, women headed 60 percent of poor family
households; two-thirds of all working women earned under $15,000
per year. Further, many of these working women were also welfare
recipients because they were unable to obtain jobs paying enough to
make the transition from welfare to work. At this first meeting,
participants explored the possibilities of creating an organization in
Chicago to assist low- and moderate-income women interested in self-
employment as an alternative to underemployment or unemployment.

From this meeting, twenty organizations became involved in the planning of the Women's Self-Employment Project. In August, 1986, WSEP initiated direct services to low and moderate income women. WSEP's orientation and Self-Employment Workshops were initiated in the fall of 1986. Gellatly contends that "over 1500 women have attended orientations, over 350 have completed the program, and 102 businesses are currently open. As of March, 1990, the loan fund had dispersed 59 loans totaling over $89,000 with only four defaults and good repayment rates" (Gellatly 1990, 3).

Within the framework of microenterprise assistance, WSEP offers both business and financial services. Included in the business services is a series of twelve small peer group training sessions which address business development skills. Upon completion of these sessions, the participants have several options. The women can start their microenterprise with funds and resources of their own; they can apply for loans to start their businesses; the application process can be postponed until a later date; or the participants can seek or maintain other forms of employment (Gellatly 1990, 5).

In the financial services, WSEP offers the Full Circle Fund, a loan opportunity based on the Grameen Bank model of peer group lending. WSEP adapted this model to meet the needs of its inner-city Chicago participants. Circles consist of women who are from the same community and are not business partners or family members. The participants must form their own circle and present itself to WSEP. Each circle must attend a four week orientation session where the members learn the rules of the Fund, the procedures for borrowing money and repayment of loans, management skills, and the endeavors of their sister members. Upon completion of orientation, WSEP certifies the circle. Once the circle is recognized, members choose two women to receive the first loans. The circle approves the women's loan proposals. True to the very basis of the Grameen Bank philosophy, WSEP participants use the trust of their Circle members as collateral for their loans; "peer pressure and support replace traditional collateral" (Gellatly 1990, 6). The first loan is limited to $1,500; the maximum Full Circle Fund loan is $5,000. Borrowers begin repayment at 15 percent interest two weeks after loan approval. Loan payments are made every two weeks. The next two members are eligible for loans after two months of consistent loan repayment from the first borrowers. After six weeks of consistent loan repayments, the fifth member becomes eligible (Gellatly 1990, 7).

Another feature of the Full Circle Fund is an enterprise or savings account to which all members deposit an agreed sum of money every two weeks. Members of a borrowing group must also contribute 5% of their loan to an Emergency fund which is used for group insurance, emergency loans to members or additional proceeds to a member's business (Gellatly 1990, 7).

The Women's Self-Employment Project, like the projects in Peru, the Dominican Republic, Kenya, India, and Bangladesh, combine group support, trust, networking, informality. and flexibility in their focus on women's economic empowerment. Also, the literature strongly suggests that an awareness of the complexities and realities of women's poverty is a significant factor in the success of these projects.

SUMMARY

This overview of research has taken a global perspective on some relevant economic development issues for poor women. A perspective of this kind is essential for the anthropologist who analyzes the development of policy on microenterprise. Aside from understanding those barriers to self-employment by low income women, it is also important to establish the idea that women are involved in multiple economic roles. Therefore, the unfolding of research on women's economic roles was discussed in this chapter. While delineating those factors which have influenced a global focus on women's economic development, this body of literature also served to validate the significance of addressing women's economic needs.

The literature on women's contributions as wage earners was also explored. This literature documented women's active participation in the work force. However, within this area of inquiry are the arguments that low income women's work choices continue to be limited, and wage work is not always an effective path out of poverty. In response to this argument, the literature review moved into scholarship related to entrepreneurship as an economic development strategy. This body of literature highlighted researchers who argue that traditional economic theorists and development specialists have typically ignored women's economic activities. This is particularly apparent in the extremely minimal research on low income women's involvement in entrepreneurship.

The anthropological and historical literature on women's autonomous economic activities across cultures documented the creative and independent ways in which women serve simultaneously as homemakers, caretakers, and breadwinners. Despite the vital nature of some women's income-generating strategies to their families, women's opportunities for expanding their businesses are often limited because they are denied credit or access to lucrative, male-dominated business domains. After reviewing the anthropological and historical literature, contemporary issues related to women and small scale business ventures were discussed. The history and structure of microenterprise assistance programs in the United States was reviewed; literature defining the concept of microenterprise was discussed; and some similarities between microenterprise and the informal economy were addressed.

In order to illustrate the economic framework within which many women build businesses, the literature review discussed the relationship between informality, microenterprise, and women's work. Several examples of Women In Development projects were provided. These projects utilize the concepts of informality, microenterprise, and women's work in economic development planning. These models provide an excellent foundation for the analysis of emerging microenterprise policy in the United States. Finally, the literature review provided an example of a domestic microenterprise assistance project which implements a Third World peer lending model. The relative success of the Women's Self-Employment Project should be considered in the development of microenterprise policy and programs in the United States. Although questions concerning the effectiveness of microenterprise as an economic development strategy for low income women will continue to emerge, this chapter has provided some evidence of the enduring nature of this concept for women. Further, this literature review addressed some of the key issues that should be considered in the formulation of policy on women, microenterprise, and economic empowerment.

III

A Look At A Microenterprise Project: Business Owners Start-Up Services

The research reviewed in the previous chapter provided some examples of successful microenterprise assistance projects. Like other microenterprise assistance projects across the nation, the Women's Self-Employment Project in Chicago, Illinois connects women's small business ownership with economic empowerment and the elimination of poverty. Although most programs in the United States are still in the research and development stages, advocates reflect an underlying sense of optimism that a reciprocal relationship of support and contribution can be developed between the microentrepreneur, her community, and the state. However, the literature also raises questions about the social and economic contexts of microenterprise training projects for women. What role does microenterprise play in the state's economic development initiatives? How does the planning of a microenterprise project reflect the needs of low income women entrepreneurs as well as the economic concerns of the state? How do the administrators of a microenterprise training project address the particular issues associated with low-income women's entrepreneurship? What important themes emerge from the participants' views on business ownership training?

These questions will be explored by describing four aspects of a microenterprise training project. These aspects include state policies, the planning, the administrators, and the participants. It was through observations and interviews with the staff and participants of Business Owners Start-Up Services (BOSS) in Baltimore, Maryland, that I was able to learn about the history and the operation of a microenterprise project, as well as the aspirations and ambitions of its participants. These are aspects of microenterprise which federal policymakers seldom experience. I wanted to understand if the work of the Select Committee on Hunger was relevant to small domestic projects. I also wanted to temporarily distance myself from the policy environment in order to develop a different perspective on the concept of microenterprise. Hence, on a very brisk February morning, I met the program director of BOSS at a designated location in Silver Spring,

Maryland, and traveled with her on a typical, forty-five minute work-day commute between Silver Spring and Baltimore. On this day, I talked to the program director as she carried out her daily work and I met the other staff members of BOSS. Also, I observed a training class, and I spoke to a group of participants who had completed training. During a second, more structured interview with the program director I learned about Maryland's role in enterprise development for low income women.

THE STATE AND LOW-INCOME EMPLOYMENT PROGRAMS

One way of viewing a microenterprise program is by looking at the state's strategies for involving low income persons in economic development. In Maryland, like other states, the majority of poor people are women and children. The median income for full-time workers in Maryland in 1989 was $18,764 for men compared with $11, 632 for women. Also, in 1989, of the 64,000 families on AFDC in Maryland, 98% were female-headed households (Maryland Department of Human Resources 1990). Recognizing the need to stimulate economic growth, as well as the need to include low-income persons in economic development planning, Maryland is engaged in a number of programs to assist welfare recipients in obtaining employment opportunities. One state-wide program which provides work and training services for AFDC recipients is Project Independence (PI). The project began on July 1, 1989. Coordinating the efforts of state and local governments and private industry councils, PI provides vocational training, education, transportation, motivational training, work experience, child care, family counseling, child support enforcement, and crisis intervention. PI's target population includes long term welfare recipients, teen parents without high school diplomas or work experience, recipients whose youngest child is within two years of becoming ineligible for assistance, and parents in their early twenties without a high school diploma or work experience (Maryland Department of Human Resources 1990, II-6).

Another state-wide program is the Food Stamp Employment and Training Program, which began in 1987. This program provides job search assistance to Food Stamp participants who are required to register for work. Another employment program which is linked to the welfare system is the AFDC-Unemployed Parent Referral to Employment Services. This program, which began in Maryland in

1987, assists principal wage earner parents who are unemployed in finding employment. The AFDC-Unemployed Parent program was created in response to a state mandate which gives priority to serving principal wage earners (Maryland Department of Human Resources 1990, II-8).

The Baltimore Self-Employment Loan Fund is another employment service for low-income persons which began in 1991. The Maryland Department of Economic and Employment Development, local foundations, and financial institutions form a private, nonprofit group which implements a revolving loan fund. This loan fund provides capital for the self-employment ventures of Maryland's low-income residents. Yet another state sponsored program is the Targeted Job Tax Credit, which provides a credit on federal income taxes to employers who hire economically disadvantaged persons, including AFDC recipients. Maryland also provides training for dislocated workers under the Job Training Partnership Act (Maryland Department of Human Resources 1990, II-8 and II-9).

Among the more recent projects in Maryland, and by far the most innovative in its attempts to provide economic options for the poor, is Business Owners Start-Up Services (BOSS). Initiated and sponsored by the Corporation for Enterprise Development (CfED), BOSS is one of five demonstration projects which constitutes the Self-Employment Investment Demonstration (SEID). CfED, a nonprofit economic development research and consulting organization, developed SEID as the first national microenterprise demonstration program in the United States. There are also SEID projects in Minnesota, Michigan, Iowa, and Mississippi. Consultants from CfED work with each state to design and operate demonstration projects which are effective in assisting welfare recipients in the development of microenterprises (Feit 1990). In July 1989, Maryland included microenterprise in its welfare reform plans. The state funded $10,000 of a planning grant, part of which was used to send two persons to observe the microenterprise initiatives in other states. Because of Maryland's interest in microenterprise, the Corporation for Enterprise Development approached the state with a proposal to join the SEID project. From this proposal, BOSS was created. The project is jointly supported by the Maryland Department of Economic Employment, the Maryland Department of Human Resources and other public and private agencies (Maryland Department of Human Resources 1990). BOSS and the other state-mandated employment and training programs represent the state's efforts to connect the provision of social services to gainful employment. Simultaneously, the state addresses the elimination of poverty and dependence. Hence, microenterprise is viewed as one of several strategies for the reduction of the state's welfare budget.

PLANNING THE DEMONSTRATION PROJECT

Another way of viewing a microenterprise training project is by looking at the planning of the project, particularly its objectives. It is important to consider how the objectives reflect the needs of the recipients/participants as well as the concerns of the state. The proposal for the BOSS project lists nine specific objectives. The first objective of the project is to develop and test a feasible model of entrepreneurship for AFDC recipients which can be replicated in other parts of Maryland. The second objective is to promote self-sufficiency through self-employment for AFDC recipients (Maryland Department of Human Resources 1990, I-1). These two objectives consider the possibility that welfare recipients have the potential to contribute to economic development, and should be supported in their creative ventures. The third and fourth objectives are to amend social service policies that hinder self-employment, and to allow AFDC recipients to receive public assistance support while starting their microenterprises (Maryland Department of Human Resources 1990, I-1). These objectives are a recognition of the inherent penalties to the poor in poverty-related policies. The fifth and sixth goals are to demonstrate the effectiveness of modest investments in microenterprises, and to create jobs in the private sector for AFDC recipients (Maryland Department of Human Resources 1990, I-1). These goals relate to the reciprocal nature of investing in the poor, who can in turn, contribute to the economy. The seventh goal is to determine the effect of the entrepreneurial experience, business skills training, and business contacts on the subsequent employability of recipients, including those whose businesses are not successful (Maryland Department of Human Resources 1990, I-1). This goal addresses the potential value of exposure to entrepreneurial culture for persons with limited experiences. The underlying belief is that entrepreneurial training can enrich people's lives and assist in finding wage work if necessary. The eighth goal is to achieve long term savings by reducing the number of years recipients rely on public assistance. The ninth goal is to achieve all objectives without increasing AFDC or medical assistance costs during the waiver period (Maryland Department of Human Resources

1990, I-1). These last two goals are related to the state's objective of limiting public assistance payments.

In its program design, BOSS is an experimental project that includes some consideration of issues related to gender, class, economics, and policy. By addressing certain restrictive AFDC regulations, providing technical assistance to participants, and developing a seed capital loan fund for business start-up expenses, the objectives speak to the inclusion of low-income women in Maryland's economic development scheme. It is also important to recognize that the state's goal of reducing welfare dependency is reflected in these objectives.

One of the most complicated aspects of planning a microenterprise training project for low income women lies in surmounting some of the restrictive barriers embedded in federal welfare regulations. Even after receiving training and support, self-employed welfare recipients cannot accumulate working capital and continue to receive public assistance. Hence, after receiving business loans, single mothers with entrepreneurial aspirations may become ineligible for assistance even before their businesses are stable enough to support a family. Through the state agency responsible for administering the AFDC program, each director of a state microenterprise demonstration project must apply for waivers of selected federal welfare regulations (Maryland Department of Human Resources 1990). Technically, the AFDC waiver is an amendment to existing welfare regulations, which changes some of the rules that threaten entrepreneurship for low-income persons (Feit and Das 1990).

The demonstration and waiver authority of the Social Security Act, Title IV-A, Section 1115, allows states to carry out experimental or demonstration projects that "promote innovative improvements in the administration and execution of public assistance and related services, or help recipients reduce their dependency" (Feit and Das 1990, 3). Section 1115 waives some of the rules and restrictions governing benefit eligibility and offers special project funding to successful state applicants. The waiver application is made to the Office of Family Assistance (OFA) in the Family Support Administration of the Department of Health and Human Services. States can also apply to the Low Income Opportunity Board, an advisory body established by Executive Order in 1987. Programs involving only AFDC waivers must be approved by OFA. However, should a demonstration project also need waivers of Medicaid, Food Stamps, and other transfer payments, the state must apply to the Low

Income Opportunity Board. Therefore, the Corporation for Enterprise Development advises microenterprise Program Directors to apply to the Low Income Opportunity Board for "a package of welfare system waivers that normally would require separate applications to the various agencies involved" (Feit and Das 1990, 3). The time involved for completing the waiver application and receiving approval demonstrates the enormity of the bureaucratic process. The waiver application is a proposal submitted by the Program Director. The proposal for waivers from BOSS is a complex ten page document involving detailed calculations of costs and benefits of the project. The average time of response from the Low Income Opportunity Board is 90 days (Feit and Das 1990, 5). However, OFA or the Low Income Opportunity Board can take up to five months to act on an application. Also, the responses are not always positive. The Corporation for Enterprise Development reports that, since 1987, only 15 of the 26 applications received by the Low Income Opportunity Board have been approved (Feit and Das 1990, 5). Further, state projects must apply for the 1115 waiver annually. Late applications could jeopardize the opening of a business (Feit and Das 1990, 5). One of the many problems faced by the first training class of Business Owners Start Up Services was that waivers were not available for the women who had prepared to open businesses.

The necessity for waivers of welfare regulations, the complexity of the waiver process, and the length of time for consideration of waivers connects microenterprise to a cumbersome bureaucratic system. Welfare recipients are once again subjected to an immense, impersonal administrative body which is driven by rigid rules. However, the ability to obtain the Section 1115 waivers also connects women's microenterprise with challenging the system and changing the rules.

THE PROGRAM ADMINISTRATORS AND TRAINERS

I was able to learn about Maryland's role in microenterprise and the planning of the BOSS program from the program director, who not only talked at length about the program, but also shared information from the Corporation for Enterprise Development and the state agencies which were monitoring BOSS. While observing the BOSS project in operation, I realized that the most important way of viewing a microenterprise training project is by looking at the people involved in the project. The BOSS staff includes a Program Director, three Business Trainers and a secretary. The small staff size requires each staff member to perform several jobs. Each Business Trainer teaches part time and assumes other necessary responsibilities. Specifically, one trainer also works as a recruiter and job developer. A second trainer serves as a community coordinator. A third trainer works as a fiscal planner for the project. The three Business Trainers form a group of professional persons who have many years of experience in social services or businesses within the Baltimore community.

The BOSS Program Director has a Masters Degree in social work. The focus of her professional life has been working with families in the United States and in other countries. She became interested in women's economic empowerment while working in the Peace Corps. During her time spent in Central America, she became familiar with the concept of microenterprise by observing the creative economic strategies which families employ to survive. In the early 1980s the Agency for International Development was funding self-sufficiency projects which supported and strengthened women's informal business activities. Experience in assisting women with traditional and nontraditional employment endeavors influenced her belief that the key to a better quality of life is economic empowerment. Although the program design indicates that 50% of the Program Director's job should be training, administrative responsibilities require most of her time. She expresses frustration with the bureaucratic demands of the job, such as designing and setting up the loan fund, writing the welfare waiver proposal, and meeting with various city and county agencies which support the project.

The educational and professional training of the staff, particularly the Program Director's social work credentials, reinforces the idea of BOSS as a social service project. One positive aspect of this is that the staff is able to address some of the personal issues which complicate business ownership for public assistance recipients. One African-American staff member attempts to connect with the African-American women who make up the majority of the class. Having worked in various social service agencies, she understands the indignities these women face as welfare recipients. In a support group formed by some of the participants, the staff member facilitates a discussion about middle-class people's perceptions of poor people's capabilities. She discusses AFDC case managers who do not inform their clients about BOSS or who attempt to discourage their clients from attending the classes. She feels that the case managers are threatened by the potential success that BOSS offers the participants.

One African-American male staff member, who is also a community leader, discusses the deceptive language of racism and classism. He tells his class that the concept of "working hard" has a different meaning for rich people than it has for poor people. He argues that, for low income entrepreneurs, working hard must mean contributing to the community. He also tells the class of predominantly African-American women that blacks have not been taught to manage businesses. As a social worker, the Program Director must counsel persons who may not necessarily be appropriate for the program, or whose goals may not be realistic. She notes that often those persons who have been employed have a more realistic sense of business ownership than welfare recipients who may have limited experience in the work force. However, she stresses that the staff "never tells anyone that their dream is wrong".

The staff's interactions with the participants on a personal level are vital to the success of the program. It is also important to look at the strategies used by the staff to initiate the first class. This shows how the BOSS staff attempted to establish a sense of the professionalism which is necessary in the business world, while also realizing the needs of their potential students. In August and September of 1990, participants for the project were recruited through community outreach and referrals. Community outreach included news articles, and radio and television announcements. Also, direct mailings were sent to eligible AFDC recipients who were enrolled in Maryland's Project Independence. Case managers for the AFDC program and the dislocated worker program were asked to inform their clients about BOSS and make referrals. Two thousand households in Baltimore City and Baltimore County were sent the bright blue flyer which boldly stated, "You Have the Power to Live Your Dreams!" The one-page advertisement included some brief information about the project and encouraged potential participants to "Start your own business and leave welfare behind!"

From the first recruiting efforts, forty-two persons attended the three hour orientation. During the orientation, applicants with specific business ideas or interests in the program were invited by the staff to attend an informational assessment workshop concerning the realities of microbusiness ownership. At the workshop participants would be prepared for the final screening. Forty persons attended the assessment workshop and met individually with the staff. During the assessment phase, eligible participants were selected based on such factors as business ideas, manageable family debts and relatively stable personal life. Thirty-six persons participated in the selection interviews, and thirty-two persons were enrolled in the first training class. Of the thirty-two participants, twenty-nine were women (Maryland Department of Human Resources 1990, III-5).

The first training and technical assistance classes took place over a twelve week period, from October 1, 1990 to December 30, 1990. The curriculum included classes on sales plans, designing a business records system, possible locations for businesses, advertising plans, opening day balance sheets and the first year revenue estimates. Participants made commitments to attend all training sessions and complete all assignments. During the twelve-week training session, participants prepared business plans which were reviewed by the trainers as well as business mentors from the community. After completing their business plans, participants prepared loan applications. BOSS assisted in identifying possible lending resources, and the participants were required to seek out their own business loans (Maryland Department of Human Resources 1990, III-5).

BOSS employs several strategies in assisting its participants with business loans. The preferred source of loans is financial institutions that are familiar with the project and are willing to provide assistance. A second possible source of financial assistance to microentrepreneurs is state and local loan funds, including Maryland Small Business Financing Authority, the Council for Equal Business Opportunity, and Development Credit Fund. These funds are operated by Maryland's Department of Economic and Employment Development, and have limited funds for state residents. A third resource for microenterprise see capital is the local community self-employment revolving loan fund which is available for the participants of the twelve-week demonstration project. The loan fund is administered by the staff of a contracting loan fund agency. Local bankers and other professionals in the Baltimore community form a loan review committee that reviews applications and approves business loans to qualified participants (Maryland Department of Human Resources 1990).

Despite the plans and goals of the project, at the end of the first twelve-week training period, there were difficulties in acquiring AFDC waivers and business loans. By February 1991, the necessary waivers had yet to be approved and none of the participants had been approved for loans. Of the thirty persons who had completed the training classes, eleven were considered to be "quick starts", meaning they were likely to begin businesses within two months. Thirteen of the participants were considered to be "delayed starts" and likely to start their businesses after four months. Six of the participants were counseled to seek wage employment after determining that microenterprise was not appropriate for them at that time (Maryland Department of Human Resources 1990).

THE PROGRAM PARTICIPANTS

Another view of BOSS is presented by the participants, most of whom are women. The participants entered the first training class with business ideas and had to become comfortable with critiques from the program trainers, as well as from consultants of the Small Business Development Center. During the training period, participants learned to describe their dream business in specific terms that helped them to face the difficult challenges that are characteristic of business ownership. By defining the target population, developing marketing strategies, and facing the realities of the competitive business world, the participants also learned about themselves.

The completion of BOSS's first twelve-week training class was a time of anxiety for the staff as well as for the participants, who were uncertain about the next steps to take in their business development plans. It was in this tenuous, ambiguous environment that six of the participants agreed to meet with me and discuss their experiences in the BOSS program. All six of the participants, three African-American and three white Americans, were young, single mothers, and public assistance recipients. After participating in the program and facing the harsh and often discouraging realities associated with low-income entrepreneurship, these young women formed a support group and met weekly at the BOSS office.

Prior to their arrival at the meeting the participants had been informed that I would be visiting BOSS to collect data for my research. Their decision to discuss their lives with me was completely optional. Thus, I would not have attended the support group without the permission of each group member. Typically, the business trainers did not attend the support group unless invited by the participants/students. However, the staff's only African-American woman business trainer also participated in the support group to make introductions and answer any questions that the women might have about my presence. This particular staff member was one in whom the group had established trust. On this day, February 27, 1991, none of the women had received the financial support necessary to begin operating the businesses they were planning. Each expressed various levels of cynicism and disappointment with BOSS. Yet each woman was still holding on to her dreams.

Despite some of the reservations expressed about talking to yet another middle-class woman about their lives, the women agreed to share some of their insights on the intersection of welfare and business ownership with me. The following paragraphs represent microseconds in the lives of women who work and wait for economic autonomy. The names used are fictitious to respect and preserve the privacy of each person involved:

Micki Taylor. Micki is a young white woman, who discussed her plans to open a janitorial service. After hearing about BOSS through her AFDC case manager, Micki decided to develop skills she was familiar with from previous janitorial work. She described some of the hardships of her life, such as marriage to a drug addict and being diagnosed as manic depressive. Micki felt that these factors led her to seek support from AFDC. Yet she also felt that her mental "handicap" would make her work harder because she wanted to prove herself to be a capable woman. Through business ownership, Micki hoped that she and her child would become self-sufficient.

Althea Yarborough. Althea, an African-American woman, exclaimed her amazement when she first read the BOSS flyer at her sister's house. It was an opportunity she had hoped for, but it sounded too good to be true. She called her case manager, who expressed the view that Althea might not be appropriate for business training classes. Althea described herself as a nonconformist who knew how to get through the system. She convinced the AFDC case worker to make the referral, and she attended the classes. Althea planned to open a bookkeeping business. She felt that her methodical personality and her ability to economize would serve her well in business development. Althea spoke of having support from a very strong, determined family. She was not ashamed of being financially supported by welfare, and said that she chose welfare as a way to remain at home with her two small children.

Dena Milgram. Dena is a young white woman, and the parent of one child. She felt that BOSS was supporting her dream of owning a mobile hair salon. Dena attended cosmetology school two years earlier and was working informally in her home. She discovered the BOSS project through a flyer in the mail. While not minimizing the training offered by the BOSS project, Dena felt that her family and friends were so extremely helpful in supporting her business endeavors. With some very specific ideas on how she would run a business, Dena expressed confidence that she would receive a loan to buy the equipment and supplies for her beauty shop.

Lisa Venetti. Lisa is a white woman in her late twenties. She spoke very candidly about the humiliation she felt when she approached a bank officer about a business loan. "What's a smart girl like you doing on welfare?' was one of the degrading remarks made by the male bank official. Lisa felt that the difficulties she faced being poor, overweight, and on welfare, were often insurmountable. Yet, she had always been interested in owning a business. In order to shape her artistic talent into a business, Lisa had set up a studio in her home, and was offering ceramics classes to her neighbors, family members, and friends. As a mother of two children who were born when Lisa was a teenager, she expressed her hopes of leaving the welfare system.

Helena Wright. Helena, an African-American woman in her early thirties, planned to open a bail bond business. She had worked for several years in an insurance office, and had saved money to start her own business. In order to learn about business ownership, Helena took a leave of absence from her job, and worked part time for friends who had a small business. After attempting to start a business using her savings, Helena realized that she would not be able to support her two children and operate a business. When she found out about the BOSS project, Helena closed her savings account and "did what [she] had to do" to qualify for AFDC. Although she expressed skepticism about the staff of BOSS and their ability to help her, Helena was certain that she would someday operate her own bail bond business.

Joanna Dunbar. The youngest member of the group, Joanna was a twenty-six year old African-American woman who discussed being on her own since she was fifteen. She had her first child at sixteen, but returned to high school and received her diploma. Joanna attended college briefly, but another pregnancy and the birth of twins forced her to leave school and live with relatives. She spoke of the difficulties of being a very young parent and attempting to work to support her children. Joanna finally applied for welfare in order to survive. She enrolled for classes with the BOSS program because she wanted to open an amusement center with video games and activities for the children in her neighborhood. Aside from her desire to own a business, Joanna also wanted to provide some structured recreation for the economically disadvantaged children in her community.

The brief stories of these six women and their relationships to BOSS give some idea of the participants' responses to Maryland's economic development initiatives. Each woman employed some type of conscious strategy, which involved confronting society and the welfare system, in order to enroll in the BOSS program. In some cases, confronting the system meant demanding or insisting upon a referral from the AFDC case manager. For all of the women, confronting the system meant challenging society's perceptions of the goals and ambitions of welfare recipients.

The words of these potential microentrepreneurs reflected their hopes and dreams, as well as the many hours that had gone into the planning and preparation for business ownership. Their words also spoke to the changing nature of women's ideas about work, and the importance of autonomous economic activities to women. Despite their poverty, or society's views on what their aspirations should be, this particular group of women wanted to make choices about the kind of work they would do to support themselves and their families. They chose business ideas based on talents or skills with which they were familiar. Some women chose business ideas that were compatible with their mental of physical health needs. In most cases, the women had been informally carrying out their business ideas for some time. However, their efforts to formalize or expand their business activities by enrolling in BOSS are indicative of their willingness to take risks. Specifically, these women could jeopardize their eligibility for AFDC, subsidized health care, and Food Stamps, if they revealed their informal business activities. Hence, aside from facing those risks which are typically associated with business development, economically disadvantaged women must also face penalties associated with poverty.

CONCLUSION

Those processes involved in the creation, formalization, or expansion of microenterprise have been explored by describing Business Owners Start-Up Services in Baltimore, Maryland. The description of this state demonstration project goes one step beyond the theoretical perspectives presented in the literature review by examining four aspects of a microenterprise training project. One perspective is that of the state government which focuses on economic growth, reduction of unemployment, and especially, reduction of public assistance payments. From the perspective of the state of Maryland, microenterprise development for welfare recipients is one of several strategies for involving eligible welfare recipients in capitalist endeavors in order to reduce their dependency on government. On another, somewhat existential level, is that perspective presented by the creation of the actual project, including the formulation of a commitment, the seeking out of funding, the development of goals for the project, and the bureaucratic procedures involved in creating and maintaining the project. The goals of the BOSS project present an idealistic view of the way a support service should work. However, the bureaucratic and cumbersome process involved in obtaining welfare regulation waivers is an affront to the very people served by the project, and may even discourage participation in BOSS.

Another perspective of microenterprise is presented by the persons who are directly involved in the administration, operation, and growth of the program. The program directors and business trainers of BOSS present a view of the strategies used by the staff to recruit, teach, counsel, and interact with the program's participants. The interweaving of social services, economics, community, and business are evident in the trainer-participant relationships. Another perspective for analysis is that of the participants. This perspective speaks to the complexities as well as the small victories inherent in microenterprise endeavors. These perspectives combine to illustrate the social and economic contexts of microenterprise for low income women. Specifically, Business Owners Start-Up Services connects business development with welfare reform, self-sufficiency, self-esteem, challenging the system, making choices, and possibly eliminating poverty for some women.

In 1991, while BOSS struggled through its formative stages, the staff of the Corporation for Enterprise Development (CfED) worked to improve the service delivery of its SEID demonstration projects. Issues related to increasing the number of business start-ups, program evaluation, and particularly the welfare waiver process, were addressed in national SEID conferences. Of primary import to CfED was the development of policies that would make demonstration projects for welfare recipients less bureaucratic, less costly, and more widespread. After consultations with various legislators who were considering the development of policy on microenterprise, the staff of CfED began working with the Select Committee on Hunger. The domestic task force of the Select Committee had committed itself to learning as much as possible about microenterprise development. In this endeavor, members of the domestic task force contacted CfED and scheduled fact-finding meetings. In these meetings, consultants from CfED described some of the most pressing problems associated with microenterprise assistance projects in the United States. Later, during the drafting of the "Freedom from Want" act (an omnibus bill that included a microenterprise component) the staff of CfED participated in every phase of the Select Committee's policy formulation process. Because of CfED, the Select Committee on Hunger began to understand some of the realities of programs such as BOSS. Because of CfED and its SEID programs, which were empowering many economically disadvantaged persons across the nation, the Select Committee on Hunger began to understand how microenterprise could be used as a tool to fight poverty.

IV

The Select Committee On Hunger: Historical, Political, And Ethnographic Contexts

Although microenterprise was a pivotal, innovative welfare reform mechanism for Business Owners Start-Up Services and the Corporation for Enterprise Development, in 1990 the issue had not gained widespread popularity in the Congress as a whole. One of the few Congressional bodies which had become involved with microenterprise was the House Select Committee on Hunger. Before addressing the Select Committee's work on this issue and the implications of microenterprise legislation for low income women, it is important to consider some of the historical and political events that shaped and defined this particular Congressional body. Hence, the first section of this chapter will present the Select Committee within historical and political contexts. It is also of the highest import to analyze the Select Committee within an ethnographic context in order to understand how the daily office interactions influence policy formulation. Therefore, the second section of this chapter consists of an ethnographic account of policy development with the Select Committee from August, 1990 to May 1991.

HISTORICAL AND POLITICAL CONTEXTS

Aside from its work on specific legislative issues, the Select Committee on Hunger has a very rich history of political events that led to the original authorization of this body. There are also some intriguing events that contributed to the survival of the Select Committee in the House of Representatives. The presentation of these events serves two purposes. First, the historical-political data compliments the anthropological data by describing origins, patterns, time, place, and continuity. Secondly, the presentation of the historical-political data contributes to a holistic description of the Select Committee by exploring some key questions. Among those questions are: What purpose does a select committee serve in Congress? What events led to the original authorization of the Select

Committee on Hunger? What early political influences shaped the legislative agenda of the Select Committee? How did the original Select Committee staff develop a legislative agenda? How did the Select Committee establish a connection to the economic lives of poor women in America? We can begin to address these questions by taking a brief glance at the history of select committees in the United State Congress

The Specialized Nature of Select Committees

Select Committees of the contemporary United States Congress are considered to be provisional, non-legislative committees. Unlike standing committees, which have the authority to consider bills and resolutions after their introduction, select committees must be reauthorized by Congress every two years and have no formal power to report legislation (Lees 1967). Historically, select committees were utilized extensively in early Congresses. Pease (1977) reports that until 1816, the majority of the Senate's legislative duties were performed in select committees. The extensive use of select committees in the early 1800s is attributed to the flexibility of the early committee system, which allowed these committees to draft legislation and make policy recommendations. Also, at that time, the creation of a select committee often insured that the majority's viewpoint would dominate, since the committee would consist of those legislators who supported the majority. However, with the emergence of the standing committee system after 1816, the Congress' use of select committees declined (Pease 1977, 6-8). In 1990, there were three select committees in the Senate (Select Committee on Ethics, Select Committee on Indian Affairs, and the Select Committee on Intelligence) and five select committees in the House of Representatives (Select Committee on Aging, Select Committee on Children Youth and Families, Select Committee on Hunger, Permanent Select Committee on Intelligence and the Select Committee on Narcotics Abuse and Control).

Usually, the creation of a select committee is triggered by the recognition that Congress, as a Committee of the Whole, is unable to effectively and efficiently address those issues related to a particular problem. Thus, select committees are created by resolutions introduced in the House or Senate. Theoretically, these committees exist for a limited time period for the purposes of investigating, studying, and reporting findings, and making recommendations to the Congress. The most significant aspects of select committees are their investigative capacities and their ability to draw public attention to specific issues through reports and hearings. Because they have no inherent legislative mandate, select committees can choose either to shape a legislative agenda or react to legislation proposed by other Congressional offices. When a select committee chooses to shape its own legislative niche, it defines itself and its constituency. Also, by shaping a legislative niche, a select committee can obtain power and possibly status as a permanent body. Despite their impermanent nature, select committees can become highly visible vehicles of power for members of Congress who serve as chairpersons.

The Authorization of the Select Committee on Hunger

When the ninety-sixth Congress initially authorized the Select Committee on Hunger on February 22, 1984, it was not the first time that a Congressional committee had been created to study the causes and effects of global hunger and malnutrition. Seventeen years earlier, in the Senate, the Select Committee on Nutrition and Human Needs had monitored and legislatively supported human service programs such as Food Stamps, the School Lunch Program, and the Special Supplemental Food Program for Women, Infants and Children (WIC). Before its demise in 1971, this Senate committee held hearings on welfare reform and other issues related to the Aid to Families with Dependent Children (AFDC) program. Like its later counterpart in the House of Representatives, the Senate Select Committee determined that the basic cause of hunger and malnutrition in the United States and in developing countries, was poverty. Also, like the Select Committee on Hunger, the Senate Select Committee determined that without radical action, hunger and poverty would continue to increase at an astounding rate. These findings would influence the legislative agendas of both Select Committees, compelling each to establish a Congressional link to the economic lives of low-income families throughout the world..

Both the Senate Select Committee on Nutrition and Human Needs and the House Select Committee on Hunger accepted the responsibility and the luxury of defining their legislative territory. However, amid an increasingly conservative Congress, the Senate Select Committee on Nutrition and Human Needs would close its doors, sending a frustrated staff of liberal-minded poverty fighters off to work for other Congressional offices, or to private nonprofit advocacy agencies. The Select Committee on Hunger would struggle to sustain a highly visible place in Congress by developing a relationship with an intricate and diverse network of grassroots advocates, and shaping a legislative agenda which also reflected the political and popular interests of the contemporary United States Congress.

Early Political Influences

Unlike the liberal political environment during the creation of the Senate Select Committee on Nutrition and Human Needs, the Select Committee on Hunger emerged in 1983 during a time of increasing political conservatism. The Senate Select Committee had participated in establishing foundations for some of the most liberal trends in the history of social service programs. Among the trends was one which allowed states the option of providing social service benefits to families headed by unemployed males. Other liberal trends included initiation of Medicaid, Food Stamps, and incremental increases in benefit levels to great numbers of person qualifying for public assistance (Piven and Cloward 1982). With Senator George McGovern as its Chair, the Senate Select Committee on Nutrition and Human Needs flourished in its policy activities during the peak of the War on Poverty.

Seventeen years later, on January 3, 1983, Democratic Representative Mickey Leland of Texas and Republican Benjamin Gilman of New York introduced House Resolution 15 to create the Select Committee on Hunger. As is the custom of the Congress, this resolution was referred to the very powerful Rules Committee, which subsequently held a perfunctory hearing on the resolution. A substitute resolution, House Resolution 20, was reported by the Rules Committee, and the House passed this resolution overwhelmingly on February 22, 1984 (U.S. House 1984).

The groundwork for public support, and indeed for a national constituency of the Select Committee on Hunger had been done by obtaining organized approval of sixty-five national grassroots organizations. Thus, by the time House Resolution 20 had come to the floor, it had the support of the "Coalition for a Select Committee on Hunger". Among the members of this diverse coalition were: the American Association for Retired Persons; American Nurses Association; Bread for the World; the Children's Defense Fund; the Food Research and Action Committee; the Hunger Project; Mexican-American Legal Defense and Education Fund; National Council of Negro Women; National Organization for Women; Private Agencies in International Development; AFL-CIO; Women's Equity Action League; and World Vision International (U.S. House 1984).

The organizing of this Coalition was significant for several reasons. First, the support of the Coalition would be crucial to the future reauthorization of the Committee. As a provisional committee, the Select Committee on Hunger was subject to the scrutiny of the Congress every two years. Critics of the Congressional Committee system, conservative Republicans, and members of powerful standing committees can challenge the necessity and value of any select committee during the reauthorization vote. The Coalition would act as a powerful body of constituents whose voices would speak to the successes of the Select Committee. Secondly, the national and international organizations of which the Coalition was composed could also have an influence on important standing Committees of Congress. Since the Select Committee on Hunger did not have legislative jurisdiction, it performed its legislative work through standing committees. Members of the Coalition had skill and expertise in networking with the chairs of powerful standing committees in order to stimulate support for the Select Committee's agenda. Thirdly, the Coalition would act as a pulse on the advocacy community. Members of the Coalition could be consulted on relevant policy issues before the formulation of significant legislation. Further, Coalition members would monitor the Select Committee's awareness of and sensitivity to specific grassroots issues.

As the Committee's legislative interests grew, so would the Coalitions' membership. By 1990, over 400 organizations representing consumer, religious, business, labor, health, farm, academic, feminist, environmental and other grassroots interests would form the Coalition supporting the Select Committee's work. The cooperative support of the Coalition spoke to the leadership, popularity and charismatic style of Congressman Mickey Leland, who became the first chair of the Select Committee on Hunger. The Congressman's enthusiasm for the Committee was fueled by political as well as humanitarian concerns. Politically, Congressman Leland, like all Members of Congress, was in search of an issue which he could call his own. After his election in 1979, the Congressman entered the House of Representatives with the intent of pursuing health issues (Crawford 1989). His participation on both the Energy and Commerce Committee and the Health and Environment Subcommittee was indicative of his commitment to health policy. However, other Representatives had taken leadership roles on various health issues. Upon realizing that no one in the House of Representatives was speaking out on issues related to hunger and malnutrition, the Congressman began to focus on domestic and international hunger (Crawford 1989). Congressman Leland's humanitarian concern was the need to keep the issue alive in the halls of Congress. In 1984, few politicians were willing to acknowledge the severity of hunger, malnutrition and poverty during an unwaveringly conservative administration. Attorney General Edwin Meese had boldly proclaimed that there was no hunger in America. Many social programs had been virtually eliminated. Thus, the creation of a Congressional Committee built on a foundation of liberal ideals was a challenge during the Reagan era, a time of invisibility for the poor.

Both the Nixon and Carter administrations had established welfare reform through changes in the Aid to Families with Dependent Children (AFDC) program. However, by proposing and implementing the most drastic and significant changes in welfare policy in recent history, President Reagan, during his first year in office, had undermined public assistance as the advocacy community and the poor had known it. By 1981, the Congress had eliminated $140 billion from social service programs over the years 1982-1984. More than half of these cuts would come from income-maintenance programs that provided transfer payments, health care, low cost housing and food. The Reagan administration also announced additional program deductions of $45 billion in 1983 and $30 billion in 1984 in order to achieve a balanced budget by 1984 (Piven and Cloward 1982). In contrast to the Nixon and Carter proposals which would have extended welfare benefits as well as the federal government's responsibilities to the economically disadvantaged, Reagan's policies severely restricted assistance to the poor (Piven and Cloward 1982).

The Select Committee on Hunger was created three years after Congress passed into law the Omnibus Budget Reconciliation Act of 1981 (OBRA). The Reagan administration's lack of empathy for the poor contributed to Congress's apathetic attitude toward domestic hunger and poverty. However, a devastating and well-publicized famine in Ethiopia strongly focused Congressional attention on international hunger issues and the need for a Congressional vehicle to demonstrate America's humanitarian concerns toward the disadvantaged in poor countries. Clearly, international concerns provided the substantive and influential data for the initial authorization of the Select Committee on Hunger.

Membership on the Select Committee on Hunger

The resolution originally authorizing the Select Committee on Hunger stipulated that the Committee would be composed of seventeen members of the House of Representatives, one of whom would be the chair. These members would be appointed by the Speaker of the House and would hold regular meetings on the third Tuesday of each month during Congressional sessions (U.S. House 1984). Despite this stipulation, committee meetings were not a typical aspect of the Select Committee's history. Rather, Select Committee meetings were usually convened by the Chair during times of Committee reorganization or in the event of some unusual circumstance. Historically, the Select Committee on Hunger was a political spotlight for its two Democratic chairs, and very few of the other Committee members attended or participated in Hunger Committee activities. Although the Select Committee's Congressional membership increased from its original seventeen members in 1984 to thirty members in 1990, only a small minority of the Committee's members attended hearings, briefings, trips, or symposia sponsored by the Select Committee. Members were kept informed of the Select Committee's legislative agenda through communications from the Select Committee staff.

Staff Structure of the Select Committee on Hunger

From its inception, the Select Committee on Hunger consisted of two discrete staffs, which were distinctive in their political goals and purposes. The Democratic staff, known as the Majority staff, reported directly to the Chair, and played a predominant role in the development of Select Committee reports, hearings, and a legislative agenda. The Republican or Minority staff, reported directly to the Ranking Minority Member (Congressman Bill Emerson of Missouri) and existed primarily to monitor and respond to the activities of the Majority staff. Each staff had its own office space. The Minority staff of three or four persons, functioned within a one-room office equipped with computers, telephones, desks, and moveable wall partitions. The Majority staff of ten to twelve professional staff persons, and often three or four unpaid interns, performed its duties within a four-room office area. Although working in adjoining offices, the original Majority and Minority staffs had very limited professional contact. However, as the Select Committee matured as a Congressional entity, the two staffs created a complimentary and amicable working relationship by collaborating on various Select Committee projects.

Both the Majority and Minority staffs were led by staff directors who were responsible for the administrative concerns of the offices. The Majority staff director communicated with the Chair, who maintained a personal legislative office (and staff) in another House

Office Building. The Majority staff director also approved all staff communications, represented the Select Committee at all high-level meetings, and accompanied the Chair on all Hunger Committee trips. The Minority staff director had similar responsibilities, although to a lesser extent.

The Select Committee's mandate to investigate the causes and effects of global hunger influenced the structure of the staffs, such that two hunger task forces were formed in the Majority office. The original international task force consisted of three persons who had experience in international issues from their work with the Agency for International Development and Bread for the World. The third international staff member had worked in the district office of a Congressional Representative. The domestic task force consisted of a former legislative assistant from Congressman Tony Hall's office who had experience with domestic welfare issues. The second domestic task force member was a former director of a state WIC program. Although these staff members had been involved in some aspects of social welfare, none had ever worked on a Congressional committee. The original Majority staff also consisted of a staff director, a communications director, a secretary/office manager, and a receptionist.

Establishing a Connection to Poor Women

During the development of its early legislative agenda, the Select Committee staff determined that the persons most often served by poverty programs, and indeed the poorest, hungriest, and most economically vulnerable people in the world, were families consisting of women and their children. Therefore, early in its formation, the Select Committee on Hunger established itself as an advocate for the welfare rights of poor women. As a highly visible supporter of the Special Supplemental Food Program for Women, Infants and Children (WIC), the Select Committee held hearings examining the effectiveness and accessibility of WIC as well as other federal food assistance programs (U.S. House 1988c). The WIC program, which receives wide bipartisan support in Congress, provides monthly food packages or food vouchers to low-income women, infants and children who are at nutritional risk. Eligible participants include pregnant and postpartum women (up to six months after delivery), breast-feeding women (up to twelve months after delivery), and infants and children under five whose income is 185 percent of federal poverty guidelines (U. S. House 1988c).

During the Select Committee's first regional hearing on June 25, 1984, in Greenwood Mississippi, and during subsequent hearings, testimony from WIC program administrators, service providers and participants were recorded. In 1988 the Select Committee issued a report entitled, "Strategies for Expanding the Special Supplemental Food Program for Women, Infants and Children (WIC) Participation: A Survey of WIC Directors" (U.S. House 1988c). This report was the result of a questionnaire developed by the Select Committee and distributed to directors of all state, territorial, and tribal WIC programs. From the responses received, the Select Committee was able to obtain information on program participation rates, funding, and barriers to participation. The Select Committee report also included recommendations for improving program management and expanding program services (U.S. House 1988c).

In 1989, the Select Committee was instrumental in securing an $8 million set aside in WIC to promote breast-feeding among low income mothers (U.S. House 1990). As the Select Committee's tenure progressed, it assumed a very emphatic role in supporting WIC. In April 1990, the Select Committee domestic staff was informed by a state WIC director of an impending shortfall in WIC which threatened to cause thousands of women, infants and children to be dismissed from the program. In May, a report written by the Select Committee informed the Congress of the serious budgetary shortfall. By July, the Select Committee had led the Congress to pass emergency legislation allowing state WIC programs to borrow from future appropriations in order that its current participants would continue to receive food. The legislation extending credit to those programs experiencing a shortfall, was introduced by Congressman Tony Hall, and passed both the House and the Senate within four days of its introduction (U.S. House 1990). Through these legislative activities, which clearly demonstrated the link between Congressional processes and the lives of the poor, the Select Committee on Hunger served as a legislative advocate for families by supporting critical parental responsibilities of low-income women. The Select Committee's involvement with WIC and other social service programs placed emphasis on women as rightful recipients of federal and state assistance. However, through the gradual inclusion of microenterprise as a part of its growing legislative agenda, the Committee would later speak to the possibility of women becoming social actors and contributors to their own economic empowerment.

Significant Issues and Events

In 1984, as the Minority staff monitored the Majority staff's activities and made certain that the Reagan administration's view was represented in reports and at hearings, Congressman Leland's staff set about the task of developing a legislative agenda. The international task force focused on primary health care in poor countries, U.S. emergency assistance overseas and the role of U.S. educational institutions in alleviating world hunger (U.S. House 1984). The domestic task force worked on the collecting of anecdotal data to document the severity of hunger in America. Supported by its Coalition of well-established, resourceful grassroots organizations, the domestic task force analyzed the effectiveness and accessibility of anti-hunger programs in urban and rural settings.

By 1989, the Select Committee on Hunger had established itself as a well-organized, highly visible and valuable investigative Congressional entity. Congressman Leland's humanitarian concerns about hunger and poverty worldwide were well-publicized in the national media. Internationally, the Select Committee became a primary resource on issue such as child survival in Sub-Saharan Africa, Nicaragua, Costa Rica and Honduras; health concerns, including the need for increased use of Vitamin A in poor countries; refugees and displaced persons; renewable energy sources and development; and the role of private voluntary organizations in United States assistance (U.S. House 1990). Domestically, the Select Committee focused its research and investigative energies on assessing the health and nutritional status of American children, improving the nutritional quality of food benefits, determining discrete population groups most vulnerable to hunger, examining methods for improving the effectiveness of assistance to single persons, and expanding the use of automated public assistance systems (U.S. House 1990). Also, because of attacks on the welfare system, the Select Committee's domestic concerns turned to preventing the dismantling of social service programs.

In August of 1989, at the end of the first session of the 101st Congress, tragedy shook the very core of the Select Committee. While on a humanitarian visit to Africa, the Chair, Congressman Mickey Leland, was killed in an airplane crash en route to the Fugnido refugee camp in Ethiopia. Accompanying Congressman Leland was the leader of the Select Committee's international task force, and fourteen other staff persons from various Congressional offices, all of whom were killed. In the hours and days marking the aftermath of this horrible and painful tragedy, significant changes in the leadership of Majority office would affect the political focus, the office dynamics, and the legislative direction of the House Select Committee on Hunger.

On September 28, 1989, House Speaker Thomas Foley appointed Congressman Tony Hall of Ohio as the Select Committee's new Chair. A Democrat from Dayton's third district, Congressman Hall was elected to the House of Representatives in 1978 (Barone and Ujifusa 1989). During his second term, he acquired a seat on the House Rules Committee. In 1984 Tony Hall was appointed Chair of the Select Committee's international task force by Mickey Leland (Barone and Ujifusa 1989). Perhaps influenced by his experiences in the Peace Corps, Congressman Hall had been on one of the few Select Committee members who had demonstrated an active interest in the Committee's issues. For example, in his Congressional District of Dayton and Montgomery County, Tony Hall persuaded farmers to permit him and other volunteers to pick crops missed in their fields by mechanical reapers and pickers. From this gleaning process, hungry people in Dayton could be fed (Barone and Ujifusa 1989). An even stronger influence in the Congressman's political life was his becoming a born-again Christian in the early eighties. His fervor for moral issues was evident in some of the legislative positions he assumed. For example, in 1988, Congressman Hall blocked a major education bill because it did not include a ban on dial-a-porn that he felt should be attached to the bill (Barone and Ujifusa 1989). Despite his obvious political enthusiasm and ambition, Tony Hall did not have the charismatic style, nor was he as well known and liked as Mickey Leland. However, as a senior member of the Select Committee, and as a member who was not Chairing any other committee, Congressman Hall received the appointment.

During an organizational meeting of Congressional members of the Select Committee on November 9, 1989, Congressman Hall appointed Congressman Byron Dorgan as Chair of the international task force. Congressman Michael Espy of Mississippi would continue in his previously appointed role as Chairman of the domestic task force (U.S. House 1990). Aside from the changes in the Committee's leadership, there were consequential changes in the Select Committee's office staff. A new staff director would replace Congressman Leland's appointee to that position. Along with Congressman Hall, the new staff director would determine further changes in the structure and composition of the staff.

THE ETHNOGRAPHIC CONTEXT

The ethnographic context consists of descriptions of those interactions and events which occurred in the professional lives of the Select Committee staff members from August, 1990 to May, 1991. It was during this period of time that I participated in the Select Committee's daily activities, observed the daily flow of the Select Committee as a whole and developed some ideas of the culture of the Select Committee on Hunger. The ethnographic context differs from the historical-political context in that it moves beyond document analysis and inquiry about past events, to descriptions of events occurring in the work lives of the staff during the research period. Moreover, the ethnographic context represents a compilation of those things seen, heard, discussed and felt by staff members as well as the ethnographer. Hence, the ethnographic context is colored by the various roles that I assumed while collecting data on the Select Committee's activities. The collecting of data began when I was interviewed by three Select Committee staff members in order to determine my appropriateness as a temporary staff member.

The Select Committee Office

I located the building that houses the Select Committee staff office after walking diagonally from the main House Office Buildings, crossing two busy Capitol Hill streets and entering the easternmost doors of House Annex II. The walk from the Capitol and the main House Office Buildings (Canon, Longworth, and Rayburn) to Annex II is not particularly long or interesting. Yet the distance is enough of a walk to make one realize how separate this building is from the hustle and bustle of daily Capitol Hill life. House Annex II, named "The Ford Building" in 1991, is not typically one of the buildings visited by tourists and celebrities who come to Washington, D.C.. The block-wide building is not majestic like the other House Office Buildings with their marble statues, gardens, fountains, and pillars. Although Members of Congress occasionally shuttle over to the Annex for meetings, no Member of the House of Representatives has a personal staff office there. Despite its separateness and relative quiet, House Annex II has been the home of some of the most influential and enduring Committees in the House of Representatives, including the Select Committee on Aging, the Select Committee on Children, Youth and Families and the Select Committee On Hunger. Tucked away on the fifth floor of the Annex, the Select Committee carried out its daily business seriously yet unceremoniously.

By August of 1990, the Select Committee office and staff had been in existence for six years. The staff had experienced a number of significant gains and losses during a span of time which is quite brief in Congressional terms. The Committee had continued to be a popular and well-respected Congressional entity, which was one of my reasons for seeking a position on the staff. The first image that I, an unfamiliar visitor experienced upon walking into the small, informal reception area of the Select Committee office in August, 1990, was that of the late Congressman Mickey Leland, gently embracing an Ethiopian child. A poem, paying tribute to the Congressman's humanitarian work, was printed on the photograph which showed Mickey Leland's ever-present flamboyant style. As I became familiar with the organizational history of the Select Committee, I saw this image as a reminder of the broad range of issues with which Congressman Leland and the staff had been concerned. I also came to understand that the photograph was a symbol of the predominant role that international issues had played in the Select Committee's initial authorization and subsequent history.

The Staff in 1990

My first visit to the Select Committee office involved an interview with the staff director and one member of each task force. At the time of my interview I did not realize the organizational and structural changes to which the staff was adjusting. Most of the people in the office were relatively new to the Select Committee or to Capitol Hill. The staff director, who had worked in Congressman Halls' office as a legislative assistant for ten years, had been on the Select Committee for about one year. Over the nine months that I spent with the Select Committee, the staff director presided over staff meetings, communicated almost daily with Congressman Hall about Select Committee business, reviewed all out-going responses to constituent mail, signed Tony Hall's name on correspondence, made administrative decisions for the office, and accompanied the Congressman on some domestic and international trips. As staff director, he held one of the most highly coveted Committee jobs on Capitol Hill. Like a good number of white males on the Hill, he had a law degree but had never practiced in the legal profession. Having been loyal to Congressman Hall for so many years, he was now reaping the rewards with a highly paid and highly responsible position in Congress. In general, the Hunger Committee's staff director had no direct involvement in the formulation of policies, even though he read every piece of proposed legislation. He maintained an amicable relationship with the staff by supporting the autonomy of each task force and distancing himself from interoffice rivalry and conflicts.

The two-person international task force consisted of one staff member who had been a junior person on that task force during Congressman Leland's leadership. After the death of Congressman Leland and the head of the international task force, this junior person was appointed the senior task force member. His coworker in international issues was a young woman who had been working for the Select Committee for six months. Both members of the international task force were white, in their early thirties, highly educated and had worked in foreign countries before coming to Capitol Hill. Despite their similarities, these two people had some difficulty working together. The reasons for this difficulty were not always clear. However, at the end of my time with the Select Committee, the senior international task force member resigned to work for an international development organization.

The two person domestic task force continued to be led by its original senior member (who had worked for Congressman Hall before becoming a member of the Hunger Committee staff in 1984). The senior member of the domestic task force, one of two African-American women on the staff, was the person who strongly encouraged me to accept a position with the Select Committee, and became the person that I reported to and communicated with on a daily basis. This particular staff member began working on Capitol Hill at the age of eighteen before earning her Bachelor's degree. Having worked in the offices of two different Congressmen over a period of ten years, she was very knowledgeable about Congress. She had not only been with the Select Committee since its inception but had written the legislation defining the very basis of the Hunger Committee. She had also planned to make the last trip with Congressman Leland, and include a visit to her mother who lived in Ethiopia. Fortunately, her plans had to be changed shortly before the trip. In August, 1990, this seasoned staff member was one of the very few people in the office who had worked closely with the late Congressman Leland. The junior member of the domestic task force, a young white male, who had recently graduated from Yale Divinity School, had been with the Select Committee for only a matter of months and was still adjusting to Congressional life.

Among the other staff members was an African-American woman who worked in the Majority office, but was also responsible for working with the Minority staff. This young woman had earned a law degree from Howard University but had never practiced law. Before becoming a member of the Hunger Committee staff, she had been a full-time homemaker, taking care of her two very small children. Her husband had been the leader of the international task force and was among those who died in the plane crash with Congressman Leland. A few months after her husband's death she sought a position with the Hunger Committee staff and was now struggling to readjust to a life that no longer held unquestioned assurances. Simultaneously, she was attempting to adjust to full-time employment and single parenthood.

The most visible and intrusive staff member was the Select Committee's Communications Director, who had recently been hired by Congressman Hall to develop press releases, write speeches, and promote an acceptable image of the Congressman to the public. The "selling" of the Select Committee on Hunger became a very prominent aspect of the staff. All legislative activities, including hearings, symposia and proposed legislation were made into news items for local and national newspapers, radio and television stations. The Communications Director also accompanied the Congressman on domestic and international trips.

Other Select Committee staff included a young man who did clerical duties and was responsible for answering the Select Committee phones which rang incessantly. There was also an office manager, who handled the Select Committee payroll and was responsible for providing clerical support services for the staff director and the two task forces. Additionally, there were two men who worked part -time as computer support personnel, and a host of unpaid interns (primarily college students fulfilling some undergraduate class requirement) who did whatever they were directed to do.

All eleven members of the permanent the staff, while adjusting to the deaths of Congressman Leland and the head of the international task force, were also involved in reorganizing and refocusing the Committee. Upon joining the staff, I became a part of the transitional stage of the Committee as I observed the rivalry between the remaining few who had been "Mickey's people" and those who were "Tony's people". The person who continued to feel much loyalty to the memory of Mickey Leland's was the senior member of the domestic task force. Although she had worked for a number of years in Tony Hall's office, this staff member had developed immense respect for Congressman Leland's leadership of the Select Committee.

She felt that as an African American who had grown up in a poor family, Mickey Leland was aggressive in the fight against hunger and poverty. She did not see this kind of passion in Tony Hall, a white American who had grown up in a rich family. In private conversations the staff member expressed her anger that most of the staff knew very little about the late Congressman. Another staff member, the widow of the former international task force head, had known Congressman Leland personally and was a close friend of the Congressman's widow. Although this staff member was committed to her work on the Select Committee, she also felt that the loss of African-American leadership on the Select Committee had changed the focus of the staff.

Partisanship in a Political Environment

Although the leadership of the Majority office was indeed Democratic, there were staff members in the Majority office who were Republicans. These two staff members, the receptionist and the office manager, did not play a significant role in the actual policy formulating process. However, it was interesting to listen to the conversations in the office that were stimulated by partisan issues. Both of these staff members were openly conservative in their views on hunger and poverty issues. They often expressed disagreement with members of the task forces concerning Hunger Committee policies.

Aside from the disagreements on hunger issues with the more conservative staff members, there were also daily discussions on other political issues. Every member of the staff was acutely aware of international and national events since a large part of the Committee's work involved reading the many newspapers and journals which were delivered to the office sometimes hourly. In fact, most conversations among the staff were of a political nature. It was a very acceptable office practice to spend most of a work day sorting through, reading and discussing information from various journals and reports. These discussions on political issues, although informal, were the same type of discussions held during the planning of Select Committee legislative activities.

Competition Among the Task Forces

During my time with the Select Committee staff, I observed the competitiveness of the two task forces. This competitiveness was serious and stimulated by the Select Committee's early emphasis on international issues. The domestic and international teams worked in separate rooms and had few professional interactions (for example, they rarely worked on hearings together and rarely attended the same legislative activities). My awareness of the rivalry became quite vivid and momentarily painful when I realized that I could not work for both task forces as the staff and I had originally agreed upon. The international team responded to my attempts at involvement with unveiled aloofness. The domestic task force indicated unequivocally that they expected my full time participating in domestic issues. Nevertheless, I was able to observe and interact with the entire staff while I participated in domestic policy activities. I also observed that members of the two task forces could work together when necessary. For example, during the formulation of the Select Committee's first omnibus bill, there were times when the task forces coordinated their legislative efforts. However, in general, the two task forces remained quite separate in terms of their issues.

Leadership Issues

In September of 1990 the 101st Congress resumed its legislative activities. Like the other staff members, I was curious about the legislative direction of the Select Committee under Tony Hall's leadership. A hint of the direction came in October of 1990 when Congressman Hall announced to the Select Committee staff his desire to introduce an omnibus antihunger bill. Although the Congressman did not specify the components of the bill, he did communicate to the staff that he wanted a highly visible bill with innovative options for the poor which he would introduce in January of 1991. The Congressman had some vague ideas on microenterprise which he had learned about during his involvement in international issues. Along with some of the other staff members, I felt that this move was an attempt by the Congressman to establish himself as a leader, to remove himself from the shadow of Mickey Leland's legacy and to shape the Select Committee's agenda into a proactive position on hunger and poverty issues. Regardless of the Congressman's motivation for wanting a bill, the staff began preparing assiduously for the task. As the months of bill formulation passed, we all learned a great deal about networking, research and cooperation. The research and policy development on the issue of microenterprise would take precedence over work on the other issues. Hence, the story of the Select Committee's policy formulation process is also the story of how Congressman Hall's quest for legislative leadership propelled the issue of microenterprise to a prominent place on the Committee's domestic agenda.

V
The Select Committee On Hunger:
Legislative Activities Related To
Microenterprise

Daily work with the Select Committee on Hunger illustrated that the policy formulation process is not necessarily linear. Particularly in its development of policy on microenterprise, the Select Committee domestic staff went through various stages of confusion, questions, staff brainstorming sessions, research, organized task force meetings, networking with consultants, drafting, writing, and rewriting. The occurrence of these stages was not necessarily sequential. Moreover, these stages of policy development occurred in the midst of ongoing Select Committee business which was quite separate from bill formulation. However, prior to discussing the Select Committee's formulation of microenterprise policy, it is necessary to present the history of the Committee's involvement with microenterprise.

Through investigations of the causes of hunger in developing countries, staff members of the Select Committee became aware that the poor lack income or income-generating opportunities. In early 1985, the Select Committee's international task force began investigating mechanisms for assisting poor people in gaining food security and in meeting some of their basic personal needs. During trips to economically devastated regions of Africa and the Caribbean, the Select Committee learned that the urban and rural landless poor engaged in various income-generating activities. The Select Committee became interested in credit assistance to microentrepreneurs, and the effect that such credit could have in raising the standard of living for poor people in developing countries.

THE FIRST HEARING ON MICROENTERPRISE

The Committee's interest in microenterprise emerged publicly in the form of a joint committee hearing on February 25, 1986. Observations and data from this hearing would provide insight for the creation of a legislative agenda on microenterprise initiative in the United States. Because this hearing laid the foundation for future legislative activities related to microenterprise, a detailed review of its proceedings is necessary. The hearing, entitled, *"Microenterprise Credit"*, was held before the Subcommittee on International Development Institutions and Finance and the Select Committee on Hunger. Emphasizing the significance of private sector economic activities, the hearing examined the role of microenterprise in the development process, and explored ways in which multilateral development banks could provide financial resources for microentrepreneurs in developing countries. Testimony on the viability of microenterprise came from witnesses who worked in grassroots development as well as those involved in multilateral development institutions. Dr. Mohammed Yunus, managing director and founder of the Grameen Bank in Bangladesh, testified on economic principles learned "not from the textbooks now but from the people around me, those who suffer through poverty and try to make a living, try to survive" (U.S. House 1986, 4).

By relating the experiences of the very poor in Bangladesh, Dr. Yunus described the origins, the philosophy and the successes of the Grameen Bank. However, the most important and relevant aspect of Dr. Yunus' testimony at the hearing was his analysis of the banking system's relationship to the poor. The idea of the Grameen Bank evolved from Dr. Yunus' awareness that the bank on the Chittagong University campus, located in an area surrounded by poor villages, did not make loans to anyone, regardless of income. This policy was based on the ironclad concept that without collateral, there could be no loans. In his testimony, Dr. Yunus questioned the necessity of the system of collateral, and viewed this system as a restriction to providing resources for the poor. "In many cases, Dr. Yunus asserted, "collateral is used to create the meek, because in reality collateral is never used for the purpose it is intended to be used" (U.S. House 1986, 6). Dr. Yunus' recommendation to the Committees was that the international funding agencies as well as the multilateral funding agencies initiate policies which would make credit available particularly to the bottom 25 percent of the population in very poor countries (U.S. House 1986, 7).

Testimony from Jeffrey Ashe, Senior Associate Director of ACCION International, reviewed the organization's ongoing projects in Latin America and in rural banks of Ghana. ACCION, International is a nonprofit development agency established in 1961, which assists local organizations in microenterprise development projects throughout the Americas. Mr. Ashe emphasized the vital capacity of extremely small businesses in generating a majority of the 120,000 jobs a day needed in the developing world by the year 2000. Moreover, Mr. Ashe testified that microenterprise represents an even larger percentage of the jobs needed for women, recent immigrants from rural areas, the uneducated, youth and the poorest of the poor (U.S. House 1986, 10).

Mr. Ashe also credited the microenterprise sector with providing the goods and services to the poor in small quantities; providing skills and entrepreneurial training; representing an appropriate low capital, labor intensive, energy saving mode of production. In addition to defining and describing the microenterprise sector, Mr. Ashe also enumerated the obstacles that affect growth, profitability and sustainability of microenterprise, including: a lack of access to institutional credit; a dependence on traditional moneylenders with lending rates ranging from twenty percent per month to twenty percent per day; a hostile policy environment that considers microenterprise activities as illegal; and a lack of access to raw materials (U.S. House 1986, 41-43).

With their prepared statements and questions, members of both the Select Committee on Hunger and the Subcommittee on International Development Institutions and Finance provided a receptive environment to all witnesses. Like most Congressional hearings, the purpose of this hearing was to educate members of Congress on the issues, to raise public awareness of the issues, and to record significant testimony on the issues. Congressional hearings also provide a record of the extent of Congressional interest in particular issues. Although members of neither Committee had specifically focused on the importance of microenterprise to women, all of the witnesses made some reference to women's roles in the sustaining of microenterprise.

The testimonies of Beatriz Harretche and OEF International were particularly valuable in informing the Committees of women's contributions to microenterprise. Ms. Harretche, during the time of her testimony, was general manager of the Banco de la Provincia de

Buenos Aires as well as Chair of the Board of trustees of the Women's World Banking. Founded in 1979, Women's World Banking programs have a global range, and promote microenterprise for women, particularly those who do not have access to conventional lending institutions. Ms. Harretche testified that Women's World Banking maintains an office in New York and twenty-four affiliate offices in twenty-three countries. As a multilateral development institution, Women's World Banking has eight guaranty programs which have been credited for a total amount of $582,000 (U.S. House 1986, 53).

The statement to the joint Committees by OEF International, a U.S. based organization which provides entrepreneurial assistance to Third World women, specifically addressed the issue of women and credit. Founded in 1947 by the League of Women Voters, and independent since 1961, OEF's programs include training, technical assistance, small enterprise development and credit for women-owned businesses. The statement by OEF informed the committees of the impact of gender in obtaining credit: "Gender, in an of itself, should not greatly affect access to credit for the normal borrower. In reality, gender does influence the ability to borrow" (U.S. House 1986, 54). OEF informed the Committees of the very distinct barriers inhibiting women's access to credit: "their work is largely unremunerated, they carry primary responsibility for home and family, they have little practice dealing with paperwork, they lack necessary collateral and in many countries they must have their spouces' signatures if they are to qualify for a loan" (U.S. House 1986, 54).

This joint Committee hearing in 1986 laid the foundation for legislative activities on microenterprise by the Select Committee on Hunger. The hearing report included prepared statements and questions by Chairman Leland as well as Congressman Tony Hall, who was Chairman of the Hunger Committee's international task force. Thus, the Select Committee on Hunger began establishing itself as an emerging authority on the role of credit assistance and microenterprise development in the alleviation of hunger in poor countries.

DEVELOPING MICROENTERPRISE AS AN ISSUE

Through a series of legislative activities in the 99th and 100th Congresses, the Select Committee on Hunger continued to pursue its interest in microenterprise development for poor people in economically disadvantaged countries. In May of 1986, a report entitled, *"Banking for the Poor: Alleviating Poverty Through Credit Assistance to the Poorest Micro-Entrepreneurs in Developing Countries"* was issued from the Select Committee. Later that same year, Select Committee members actively supported a resolution introduced by Select Committee member, Congressman Benjamin Gilman to direct local currencies generated by the U.S. government's Food-for-Peace Program to support microenterprise activities (U. S. House 1987, v).

In October of 1986, the Select Committee sponsored a Congressional forum on credit to the poor. Panelists included Dr. Mohammed Yunus, and representatives of the Inter-American Development Bank, the African Development Foundation, the Pan-American Development Foundation and the Agency for International Development (AID). In March of 1987, the Select Committee held a hearing to examine the role of nongovernmental organizations in providing credit for the poor. The hearing also provided a forum to discuss AID's microenterprise credit efforts. Also in 1987, the Select Committee supported legislation introduced by Representative Gilman to expand funding for credit programs by AID and multilateral development banks (U.S. House 1987, v).

Although these legislative activities received recognition and support from some grassroots organizations, the international scope of the hearings, the forum and the proposed legislation did not capture the imagination of grassroots hunger advocates who were concerned about domestic hunger issues. Domestic advocates working to improve poor people's access to food and governmental assistance were not receptive to microenterprise as a method for poverty alleviation, nor were they supportive of the idea that business development could be effective in the economic empowerment of the poor. Moreover, persons working on urban and rural poverty issues appeared to be relatively unreceptive to Third World models of credit assistance to the poor. Nevertheless, astute observers committed to microenterprise projects in developing countries had begun to question the U.S. government's efforts in providing assistance for its poor. Among the early recommendations to the Congress during the joint committee hearing in 1986, was a statement by Jeffrey Ashe, of ACCION, International, encouraging domestic involvement in microenterprise:

> In conclusion, I think the Congress should consider what the lessons learned abroad in developing countries imply for this country as well. Here in this country we have a Small Business Administration that virtually does not reach small

businesses, and we have a banking sector which
virtually ignores the needs of small enterprises. I
think it would be interesting to speculate what would
a banking system be like in this country if a certain
percentage of loans were required to go to tiny
enterprise. I think the impact in this country for
alleviating rural and urban poverty would be
significant (U.S. House 1986, 12).

THE SELECT COMMITTEE AND DOMESTIC MICROENTERPRISE

Perhaps the statement by Mr. Ashe as well as the political
expediency of a domestic focus for this issue were the impetus for a
Select Committee staff report in December of 1987 entitled, *"Access
and Availability of Credit to the Poor in Developing Countries and in
the United States"* (U.S. House 1987). This report represented the
Select Committee's first comprehensive effort at investigating
microenterprise credit programs in the United States. By reviewing
testimony from the *"Microenterprise Credit"* hearing of February
1986, members of the Select Committee's domestic task force were
able to formulate questions about the feasibility of microenterprise as a
self-help strategy for poor people in the United States. In order to
gather data on domestic microenterprise issues, the domestic task force
reviewed reports from other governmental agencies such as the
General Accounting Office. News articles and unpublished reports
from community organizations provided both anecdotal as well as
quantitative data on individual microentrepreneurs and entrepreneurial
assistance projects for low income persons (U.S. House 1987).

A significant amount of information on domestic
microenterprise programs was obtained from the Corporation for
Enterprise Development (CfED). It was at this time that the Select
Committee domestic staff began to build a working relationship with
Robert Friedman, President of CfED, who provided much of the first
hand information on the issue. Mr. Friedman and his staff would later
play a very pivotal role in the Select Committee's policy formulation
process. However, in 1987, the domestic staff focused on educating
themselves about self-employment for the poor; understanding the
framework and mechanisms of some of the existing microenterprise
assistance projects; and developing a political posture on this relatively
new issue.

A substantial part of the Select Committee's 1987 report included analyses of the need for credit assistance in developing countries, case studies of microenterprise credit projects in developing countries; and Select Committee recommendations for microenterprise credit programs abroad. The inclusion of a domestic component in the report illustrated the Select Committee's attempt to address the needs of potential microentrepreneurs in the United States.

The report acknowledged the potential entrepreneurial skills and talents which are often untapped in low income communities. The report also acknowledged the viability of self-employment as an option in the reduction of the domestic unemployment rate. Although critics of self-employment for the poor cite high rates of business failures among very small businesses, the Select Committee reported that nine out of ten business failures occur due to undeveloped management skills (U.S. House 1987, 20). The report argued that through credit assistance and managerial training, microenterprise support projects reduce the failure rate among these very small businesses. By offering examples of some conventional and nonconventional microenterprise assistance programs, the Select Committee report supported domestic microenterprise initiative and validated the efforts of low income microentrepreneurs (U.S. House 1987, 20-21).

During a time when the concept of microenterprise was known to relatively few community workers and public officials, this initial report by the Select Committee on Hunger was of considerable value in the identification and description of six specific microenterprise projects. Those projects described included: The Self-Help Association for a Regional Economy (SHARE) in Great Barrington, Massachusetts; the Small Business Development System (SBDS) in Boston, Massachusetts; the Women's Economic Development Corporation (WEDCO) in Minneapolis/St. Paul, Minnesota; the Women's Self-Employment Project (WESP) in Chicago, Illinois; the Center for Southeast Asian Refugee Resettlement (CSEARR) in San Francisco, California; and the Small Business Venture Program in Boone, North Carolina (U.S. House 1987, 22-27). The domestic staff chose to analyze and describe these projects due to the innovative nature of their approach to fighting poverty. In addition, the Select Committee report described some possible sources of credit assistance for low income persons, including: Linked Deposit Programs, "Socially Responsive" Investments, Community Loan Funds, the Shorebank Holding Company, Government sponsored secondary markets, private secondary markets, and projects leveraged through the Community Reinvestment Act (U.S. House 1987, 27-32).

The report also mentioned Small Business Incubators, facilities which house very small developing businesses, allowing the enterprises to share common business necessities such as accounting, copying and mailing (U.S. House 1988, 27).

The Select Committee report also discussed the use of public transfer payments (such as AFDC benefits) as investment capital for microenterprises. Citing examples from French and British programs in which unemployment benefits are used as entrepreneurial capital, the report supported the possibilities inherent in this "speculative" concept (U.S. House 1987, 32-34).

This report represented the Select Committee's first investigation into domestic microenterprise initiatives. Thus, recommendations were general and based on the domestic task force's relatively limited experience with the concept of microenterprise. One of the Select Committee's recommendations was that the Small Business Administration (SBA) work with Community Development Credit Unions (CDCU) in order that CDCUs become involved with the SBA's guaranteed loan program. The rationale for this recommendation was that CDCUs were more flexible than other lending institutions, and could extend smaller loans for microenterprises. Another recommendation was that the SBA work directly with community microenterprise assistance projects. A third recommendation was that the Congress continue its support of the six million dollar Community Credit Union revolving loan fund administered by the National Credit Union Administration. This recommendation was based on the Select Committee's awareness of the role of credit unions in economic development as well as the specialized services provided by these institutions. The other recommendations were general appeals to the Small Business Administration, traditional financial institutions, state and local governments, and investors to encourage and support microenterprise in economically disadvantaged communities (U.S. House 1987, 34-35).

In contrast to the liberal views expressed by the Majority staff, the Minority staff of the Select Committee presented a fairly cautious and conservative stance on the issue of domestic microenterprise. With a one-page rebuttal at the end of the 1987 Staff Report, the Minority Staff suggested that there was a need for much more data on domestic microenterprise before the Select Committee actually made substantive recommendations. The Minority report argued for careful management of microenterprise lending programs, and expressed concern for the effects that microenterprise lending could have on financial institutions. Further, the Minority report defended those lending policies of financial institutions which make microenterprise lending almost impossible:

> We are concerned that this report creates the impression that financial institutions are unfairly placing some individuals or firms in a high-risk category; in fact, there may be very good and valid reasons for such determinations (U.S. House 1987, 37).

The Minority staff also expressed concern about the Majority's discussion of "Socially Responsive Investments", indicating that the Majority may be presenting a distorted view of the nature of social responsibility in financial matters. Emphasizing the educational and legislative importance of formal hearings on microenterprise, the Minority staff argued in favor of such hearings in coordination with the Committee on Banking, Finance and Urban Affairs (U.S. House 1987, 37).

The 1987 report, *"Access and Availability of Credit to the Poor in Developing Countries and in the United States"*, initiated the Select Committee's efforts in comprehending the essence of self-employment as a means of economic independence for those who would not ordinarily have the opportunity. As the report was distributed to Members of Congress and interested community development agencies, the Select Committee staff received responses in the form of telephone communications, letters, and personal visits to the Committee office from persons interested in the issue. Moreover, Select Committee staff members received information on the progress of existing microenterprise projects and the emergence of new projects. This growing body of information on microenterprise initiatives across the nation would be used in the development of future legislative endeavors. Augmenting the staff's interest in microenterprise was the development of professional expertise and sophistication in this issue. Hence, the Select Committee's 1988 *"Progress Report"* included a review of two staff reports and one hearing, all of which addressed the issue of domestic microenterprise (U.S. House 1988b).

MICROENTERPRISE AND THE ALLEVIATION OF DOMESTIC HUNGER

In its quest to present the many complex causes of hunger, the Select Committee argued, in its 1988 *"Progress Report"*, that poor individuals usually have less education, inadequate housing, and may be forced to live in less sanitary conditions. Because the poor usually have less access to financial resources, they frequently suffer from or are vulnerable to hunger (U.S. House 1988b, 62). The Select Committee report argued that staff contacts with poor persons revealed a vast majority of individuals seeking viable alternatives to public assistance. The report reiterated the Select Committee's support of microenterprise as a strategy for fighting hunger and poverty. Also, the report reviewed Committee actions on this issue, including the December 1987 report, *"Access and Availability of Credit to the Poor in Developing Countries and the United States"*; and a hearing on April 20, 1988, entitled *"Self-Employment for the Poor: The Potential of Microenterprise Credit Programs"* (U.S. House 1988b).

The Select Committee's 1988 hearing on innovative economic options was held in Washington, D.C., and examined the feasibility of microenterprise to low income families. Among the witnesses were Robert Friedman, founder and President of the Corporation for Enterprise Development; and Paula Mannillo, Director of Finance, Women's Economic Development Corporation, both of whom were stalwart proponents of microenterprise assistance for economically disadvantaged women (U.S. House 1988b, 22).

In 1988 the Select Committee on Hunger also issued a report on self-help programs entitled, *"Self-Help Programs: Innovative Options for Achieving Self-Sufficiency"* (U.S. House 1988d). A questionnaire, prepared by the domestic staff and mailed to directors of self-help programs in twenty states, provided the basic data for this report. The survey was designed to develop a sense of the nature and scope of self-help programs, and to elicit suggestions from directors on the needs of such programs. Thirty-four completed questionnaires were returned to the Select Committee between November 11, 1986 and March 27, 1987 (U.S. House 1988d, 1).

Among the respondents to the questionnaire was the Ms. Foundation for Women, a national non-profit organization which funds women's income-generating projects. The Ms. Foundation's response to the survey indicated that the organization had made grants, ranging from $2,000 to $10,000 available to groups such as

Mountain Way Herbs and Arts, a women's cooperative located in Tennessee, which produces and sells Appalachian crafts. The Select Committee also received a response from Homeworkers Organized for More Employment (HOME), a craft store established in the late 1960s by nuns attempting to provide income generating activities for themselves and other poor families in rural Maine (U.S. House 1988d, 8-9).

Although the Select Committee's activities related to microenterprise were a very small part of its agenda between 1984 and 1988, the Committee had established a clear position in support of domestic microenterprise lending, microenterprise credit, microenterprise as a self-help strategy, and the use of transfer payments as financial support for microentrepreneurs. The role of the very small business in the economic empowerment of poor women had come to the Select Committee's attention in the form of a substantial body of media information on the Grameen Bank, its philosophies and operational mechanisms. Additionally, there were increasing sources of policy research on multinational lending institutions in developing countries, as well as the literature from AID on Women in Development. Thus, an issue which was initially an international concern became a visible aspect of domestic concern. However, the Select Committee had taken no direct action in the form of policy on microenterprise, nor had it seriously considered addressing economic development concerns which were specific to poor women.

FORMULATING POLICY ON MICROENTERPRISE

In October, 1990, when Congressman Hall requested that the Select Committee develop an omnibus bill, very little had been done on the issue of domestic microenterprise since the Committee report in 1988. Although the domestic staff was certain that one component of the bill would address microenterprise initiatives, there were myriad questions and concerns in the minds of the entire staff about the process of developing legislation. Only one staff member had ever actually participated in the development of a bill. This particular staff member of the domestic task force felt that it would be wiser to hold hearings, and thoroughly research some of the issues before attempting to formulate legislation. There were concerns about "rehashing" old issues. What new hunger issues could be addressed in such a large bill? There were privately expressed concerns about the Congressman's motivation for introducing such a high profile bill. How serious was

Tony Hall about getting the bill passed? Did Tony Hall have a specific strategy in mind for passage of the bill? Further, there were concerns about the time frame and the feasibility of gathering sponsorship for the bill. Would the staff be able to hold meetings with staff members of critical cosponsors during December, a time of the year when most Representatives return to their districts? Also, how much constituency support from the advocacy community could be gathered in such a short period of time?

These questions and many more concerns became a part of daily interactions as staff members attempted to grasp the concept of an omnibus bill. The first strategy of the domestic task force was the assignment of specific issues to task force members. Four members of the task force (including myself) would research relevant issues for possible inclusion in the bill. Because the legislative agenda of the domestic task force was well established, each staff member had attained various levels of expertise on specific issues. In fact, the responsibility for specific domestic issues had been mutually agreed upon and neatly divided between those two staff members who worked only on domestic hunger issues. The leader of the task force, who had worked on the Committee since its inception, had actually developed legislative skill on most domestic issues. However, she was primarily responsible for Food Stamp policy, AFDC policy, issues related to gleaning, and elderly nutrition. The second member of the team worked on WIC, rural hunger issues, and microenterprise. A third, newly employed staff member worked partially on domestic issues and partially on international issues. This staff member's role with the domestic task force was the development of initiatives on infant mortality. As a fourth staff member, with a research agenda that included observing and participating in Select Committee activities, particularly those related to women and microenterprise, I was assigned the tasks of contacting experts and consultants on microenterprise, investigating ongoing projects and scheduling meetings with consultants. I was also assigned the task of writing the "Findings" sections of various components of the bill. (The "Findings" section precedes the actual legislative language of a bill and describes the issues involved as well as the necessity of the legislation). Additionally, each staff member of the domestic team would research their specific areas of interest, review any previous Congressional actions on the issue, and collect names of possible contact persons for consultation.

On November 8, 1990, the domestic task force held its first official meeting to discuss the omnibus bill. The first item on the agenda was the Select Committee's report for 1989. The task force team leader reminded her staff that at the end of each Congress the Select Committee must produce a report detailing its activities for that period. Members of the task force were requested to submit descriptive paragraphs on the activities for which they had been responsible during the last Congress. Included in these activities were a symposium on the role of breast feeding in reducing infant mortality, and a hearing on the poverty line. The task force leader suggested that some aspect of these issues might be included in the omnibus bill, the drafting of which was scheduled to be completed by January of 1991. During the course of this first formal meeting, task force members contributed suggestions on other issues for possible inclusion in the bill. An initial strategy was to develop the bill in tandem with the Select Committee's agenda. Thus, if introduced in January, the bill would set the Committee's "theme" for the subsequent Congress. Task force members discussed their individual areas of concern, and how these interests could enhance the bill. There was talk of a component of the bill which would speak to reducing infant mortality. There was talk of the inclusion of a methodology for the measurement of hunger in vulnerable communities. There was talk of innovative options for self-sufficiency, and, for the first time since 1988, the issue of microenterprise resurfaced on the Committee's agenda as a tool for fighting hunger in America.

Research on the issue of microenterprise, including a review of previous Select Committee activities, consultation with grassroots advocates on the issue, and the collection of emerging academic literature and media publications, would be done by the junior member of the domestic task force who was relatively new to the Congressional environment. However, having an astute understanding of the value of networking, as well as an understanding of the power of a Congressional Committee, the staff member began establishing relationships with influential persons of the microenterprise advocacy community.

Almost immediately after the first task force meeting, the staff member contacted Robert Friedman, president of the Corporation for Enterprise Development. From his office in California, Mr. Friedman presented a broad framework from which the Select Committee could work on its microenterprise legislation. In his initial considerations of what the microenterprise component of the bill would include, Mr. Friedman addressed his concerns about the barriers facing welfare recipients who attempt to create legitimate businesses. He spoke of the need for waivers of welfare regulations at the federal level. Mr. Friedman also spoke to the possibility of writing legislation which would include microenterprise as an option in federal job training programs such as those programs associated with the Job Training Partnership Act. One of the most significant suggestions made by Mr. Friedman was that the Select Committee think about microenterprise within the context of economic development. While the junior member of the domestic team consulted Mr. Friedman, I contacted Rona Feit, also of CfED, in Washington, D.C., and scheduled a consultative meeting in which the entire domestic team could participate. This contact with consultants initiated new thoughts about the role of microenterprise in poverty alleviation.

At this point in the formulation of ideas for the omnibus bill there were far more questions than answers; much more confusion than clarity. Ideas for the bill, the Select Committee's possible themes for the 102nd Congress, and supportive legislative activities continued to materialize. For example, suggestions for possible hearing or symposia topics included: "Teen Pregnancy and Infant Mortality"; "Poverty and Access to Health Care"; "Workfare and Hunger"; Reducing Food Costs in the WIC Program"; "Environmental Policy and Hunger in America"; and "Asset-Based Welfare Policy: Individual Development Accounts". These topics spoke to the Committee's legislative concern with the quality of life for vulnerable groups. In general, many of the proposed topics were issues with which the Select Committee had established some level of political comfort. By far, the most inchoate issue for the domestic task force, and indeed the issue requiring the most research, but holding the most substantive promises, was microenterprise.

On November 11, 1990 the domestic task force met with Rona Feit and Sheila Das of the Corporation for Enterprise Development. These two women had been involved in the creation of the Self-Employment Investment Demonstration (SEID) project, a four year, multi-state initiative. The Select Committee staff was informed about SEID's goal to determine the viability of self-employment as a route to self-sufficiency for welfare recipients. SEID also sought to determine if states could create an effective support system for these self-employment efforts, and if so, what barriers needed to be addressed. The staff was also informed that in 1988 SEID projects were initiated in Minnesota, Maryland, Michigan, Iowa, and Mississippi. The staff of the Corporation for Enterprise Development and a team of microenterprise consultants worked with each state to obtain waivers of welfare regulations and to design and operate pilot programs that would be effective in assisting welfare recipients in becoming self-employed within the limited time-frame imposed by the waivers. In the afternoon meeting at the Select Committee office, Ms. Feit and Ms. Das, with years of experience in dealing with the issues, enlightened the staff on the needs of microentrepreneurs, including support services, access to capital and training.

Ms. Feit briefly discussed some of the regulatory obstacles faced by microentrepreneurs, particularly women who are welfare recipients. Among the problems is the possible loss of AFDC, Food Stamps and Medicaid for welfare recipients who acquire assets. There are also zoning problems for home-based businesses. Further, eligibility requirements for loans make it difficult to tap many kinds of financial resources. As far as resources are concerned, Ms. Feit argued that there were many potential sources of capital for microenterprise, including Community Development Block Grant money; revolving loan funds; the Small Business Administration; and the Women's Business Ownership Act. Ms. Feit also mentioned the proposal of a "Micro Bank" and the feasibility of offering tax preferences to persons who invest in microenterprise.

Ms. Feit informed the Select Committee domestic staff that microenterprise lending is very individualized, so there must be a way to decentralize and provide technical support for microentrepreneurs. The staff was encouraged to think of microenterprise as a movement for which a good deal of grassroots support could be garnered. Ms. Das indicated that through working with the SEID projects, CfED learned the critical value of peer-support networks and the need for more experimentation with that concept. Finally, the staff was left with some questions to ponder in the development of legislation on microenterprise: How do we encourage the adaptation of the banking culture to the microenterprise idea? How do we work on changing attitudes about the economic transition of the poor? How can we make it easier for microenterprises to have benefit structures? Should the focus on microenterprise legislation be urban or rural? Do we want to think about microenterprise as self-sufficiency or supplemental?

The meeting with Ms. Das and Ms. Feit provided the Select Committee domestic staff with a framework for formulating ideas about microenterprise. Although the Select Committee had been involved in some microenterprise activities, the formulation of legislation was considerably more complex than writing reports or organizing hearings. There were many considerations about potential microenterprise projects including funding and administration. Nevertheless, by mid November, the domestic staff had committed itself to supporting the idea of microenterprise through some kind of legislation. That commitment was expressed in the Committee staff's first meeting with a major advocacy organization which was also a member of the Coalition for the Select Committee on Hunger.

On November 29, 1990 the staff director, the communications director, and members of the domestic and international task forces met with seven staff members of Bread For the World, a Christian-based organization concerned with global hunger and poverty issues. Although "Bread" was very much involved with issues related to the Horn of Africa, El Salvador, the reduction of military spending and Congressional budget priorities, the organization was also very enthusiastic about any hunger legislation which would reawaken the public's concern. The staff of Bread for the World was curious about Congressman Hall's vision for the bill and how Bread's needs and the Select Committee's needs could be united.

In a brief, but well-planned introduction to the meeting, the Select Committee's staff director explained that the prospective bill was a visionary one which would guide the Select Committee's actions through the decade of the nineties. He also contended that the legislation would inform people about what can be done to fight hunger in all communities. After the staff director's introduction, the international task force presented some general ideas on the international components of the bill. The Hunger Committee's international concerns would be expressed in the bill by addressing the issues of: food as a human right; the eradication of unnecessary illness, suffering and death; the environment, hunger and poverty; support for U.S. based private voluntary organizations; and women in development. Despite past involvement with international microenterprise, the international task force would not address this issue in the bill. The international task force felt that there was no need to revisit this issue since international microenterprise programs had been established in many countries.

The domestic task force presented some ideas on the envisioned components of the bill. Although WIC, Food Stamps, and other social programs would be mentioned in the language of the bill, the domestic focus would be on thinking about the future beyond these programs. Thus, it was explained that the legislation sought to initiate activities which the staff felt would eventually be more responsive to poor people's needs. As such, the bill would present a long term vision by providing alternatives for the poor. The domestic staff explained that their portion of the bill would include, among other things, comprehensive strategies for reducing infant mortality; ways of enhancing food purchasing power for the poor; strategies for improving community involvement in transition programs; and the development of microenterprise projects. Having only limited knowledge about the concept, the Bread for the World staff had several questions about the domestic staff's proposals on microenterprise. The domestic task force indicated that domestic microenterprise represented one strategy for escaping welfare dependency. The staff also felt that although models from other countries would be used in the development of pilot projects in the United States, domestic programs needed to be more comprehensive than most international projects, especially in the area of technical support. The task force also expressed the view that microenterprise funds must be attainable at the community level and allowed to grow at the community level.

The Hunger Committee's meeting with Bread for the World represented the staff's commitment to working with grassroots organizations toward the formulation of relevant and effective social policy. Committee staff members would continue to meet individually or collectively with nongovernmental agencies in consultation about the bill. The domestic task force also had several meetings with the Congressional Research Service (CRS), a governmental research body which works specifically for the United States Congress. Located on Capitol Hill in the Library of Congress, CRS provides research services on any topic requested from a Congressional office. Therefore, in the formulation of policy on domestic microenterprise, the Select Committee staff looked to CRS for information on possible sources of funding and administration of such projects.

In a meeting with the Congressional Research Service on December 6, 1990, the domestic team learned that two microenterprise bills had been introduced in the last Congress. Both Representative Barbara Kennelly, a Democrat from Connecticut, and Representative Cardiss Collins, a Democrat from Illinois, had introduced legislation which would assist with the development of microenterprise programs in their respective states. This new information alerted the staff to review these bills, determine their status in Congress, and determine if these two Congresswomen would be supportive of Congressman Hall's omnibus legislation. During the meeting with CRS, the domestic team was also advised to expand self-employment opportunities within currently existing programs such as Job Training Partnership Act (JTPA) and Aid to Families with Dependent Children (AFDC), so as not to create more bureaucracy. The feasibility of working within certain programs was discussed as well as some of the stipulations and regulations of these programs.

By mid December of 1990, the domestic staff had collected substantial information on microenterprise and formulated four basic plans for approaching legislation on the issue. One policy idea was termed the "one-percent plan", which targeted one percent of all grant and economic development finance programs for microenterprise credit programs. The focus would be on loan guarantee programs, direct loan programs, grant programs, and technical assistance programs for low income persons. There would be flexibility in the types of microenterprise programs from state to state, however, no new revenues would have to be required in order to set up the programs. For example, some states could use one percent of their economic development funds to establish "Peer Lending Programs", while other states could develop Small Business Development Centers. Among the programs or departments cited for possible targeting were: the Economic Development Administration of the Department of Commerce; the Office of Community Planning and Development through which Community Development Block Grants could be targeted; the Department of Health and Human Services through which Community Services Block Grants could be tapped; the Farmers Home Administration, administered by the United States Department of Agriculture; and the Department of Defense, through which Community Economic Adjustment grants could be targeted. Other possible resources for the development of microenterprise included: the Appalachian Regional Commission; the National Credit Union Administration; the Department of the Interior, through which grants for Native American economic development could be targeted; and the Employment and Training administration of the Department of Labor.

Another policy idea discussed by the domestic team was the inclusion of self-employment as an option within current employment and training programs. The strategy would be to extend the rules of these programs (if possible) and provide more funds for credit and technical assistance. At least three types of programs could be targeted: programs administered by the JTPA; programs under Job Opportunities and Basic Skills (JOBS); and the Employment and Training Provisions of the Food Stamp Program. However, it was clear that there needed to be more investigation into the employment needs of the populations served by these programs as well as the programs' success, goals, and strategies.

Yet another policy plan from the domestic team in the development of ideas for possible legislation was the use of public transfers as investment capital. Public transfer payments included such benefits as Social Security, unemployment insurance, and Aid to

Families with Dependent Children. Recipients of these types of federal assistance, particularly women who receive AFDC, are restricted in the kinds of independent economic activities in which they may engage. The accumulation of capital over a certain dollar amount could disqualify the recipients from receiving benefits. The task force was aware that some demonstration projects promoted self-employment through providing waivers of public assistance regulations. The Select Committee's involvement with waivers could be to make them less complicated and available in all states. The models for the development of policy on waivers could be the Self-Employment Demonstration Project (administered by the Corporation for Enterprise Development) and demonstration programs through the Department of Labor, which allowed unemployed persons to receive unemployment benefits in lump sums for the purpose of starting a business.

A fourth policy idea for consideration was the development of ten one million dollar grants to ten states for the establishment of microenterprise credit programs. This plan would require the federal government to appropriate one million dollars each to ten states for microenterprise for the poor. States would be required to match the one million dollars, but could design programs which would meet the needs of their specific populations. Granting of the funds would be competitive. Those states demonstrating the best capacity to administer a microenterprise credit program would receive grants. This plan would include a formal evaluation of each state's program at specific intervals of time.

These policy ideas instituted the basic framework for the formulation of policy on microenterprise, and would guide the domestic staff as they hastened to meet a January deadline for the introduction of a bill which by December, was still in the development stages. As work on the prospective legislation progressed, Chairman Hall was informed regularly of the status of his omnibus bill. Although the Congressman rarely visited the Select Committee office, he was accessible to the staff. In fact, staff members often held meetings with him in his Congressional office, which was located in another Capitol Hill building. The Congressman made frequent phone calls to the Select Committee office for discussions with various staff members about the bill and ongoing Select Committee issues. One particular phone call early in the conceptualizing stage of the bill, demonstrated the Congressman's eagerness to become involved with microenterprise. He called the Select Committee office with the suggestion that one member of the domestic task force accompany him on an upcoming trip to Bangladesh. The Chairman felt that a visit to the Grameen Bank would provide first hand knowledge of microenterprise credit in action, and provide insight for the formulation of policy on domestic microenterprise. Although the trip to Bangladesh never materialized due to military aggressions in the Persian Gulf, research preparation for the trip inspired some exciting ideas about the value of microenterprise efforts in the United States.

In December the Chairman was informed that the bill would not be drafted before the Congress left for recess. However, there was still some optimism about the possibility of a January introduction. When the Congress returned to Washington in January of 1991, the Select Committee staff continued its work on the development of a bill which would be far-reaching in its scope. On January 2, 1991, a memorandum was distributed to the entire staff from the communications director on the need for producing documents to support the introduction of the bill (temporarily named the HALL ACT). A pre-introduction, "problem-based" document was planned. This document would highlight those hunger problems that the bill would address. The plan was to mail the pre-introduction document to persons on the Select Committee's mailing list approximately ten days prior to the introduction of the bill. At this time, there was no definite date on when the bill would be introduced. However, a plan for eliciting support had to be in effect.

On January 8, the members of the domestic and international teams met with the staff director to discuss the progress in formulating the HALL ACT. However, there were other issues with which the Select Committee had to concern itself. On that same morning, the Washington Post had featured an expansive news report on fraudulent use of Food Stamps. The general feeling from the staff was that the article would set the Food Stamp Program back a few years. "We will be battling this article for months to come", commented one Select Committee staff member. The issue of the Select Committee's reauthorization was also a subject of mild concern. Although there were no strong indications that the Select Committee's tenure was in danger, until the reauthorization vote on the Congressional floor, Committee plans could not be finalized. There was no specific date or time announced for the vote. Therefore, the Committee's work would continue, but dates for hearings and other legislative activities could not be set since, technically, no Select Committee activities could take place before the reauthorization.

On January 15, 1991, the first public reference to the bill was made to an audience of people who had gathered to discuss the nutritional needs of children. Congressman Hall was the keynote speaker at the annual Public Voice Conference on Children and Nutrition in Washington, D.C. In his address to the group, Congressman Hall referred to the "Freedom from Want Act" as a bill which would provide options for economic self-sufficiency for the poor. In a very general description of the bill's provisions, the Congressman indicated that among other things, the bill would assist in the development of microenterprise credit programs for the poor. This first public announcement of upcoming legislation captured the attention of many in a room full of seasoned advocates, who took notes on the Congressman's comments.

In the ensuing weeks, the Congressman made several public announcements about his proposed legislation. In speeches prepared by the Select Committee's communications director, Congressman Hall explained that the bill was named in honor of President Franklin D. Roosevelt, an innovative leader who had compassion for the poor. In his state of the union message on January 6, 1941, President Roosevelt had designated "Freedom from Want" as one of the four basic freedoms of Americans. To audiences composed primarily of people who had worked for years on standard poverty programs, Congressman Hall attempted to sell his ideas on innovative options for the poor. As word about the impending legislation spread throughout the advocacy community, the Select Committee office was inundated with calls and inquiries about various components of the bill, which was still in the formulation process.

By the end of January, policy ideas on the international and domestic components of the bill were being shaped into the language of legislation. However, hopes of a January introduction were abandoned as the technical aspects of this monumental task were refined. On January 30, 1991, both task forces met with the staff director and mutually agreed on the possibility of introducing the bill during the week of February 18th or the week of February 25th. The staff director recommended that the Select Committee staff talk to the staffs of Republican leaders as well as the staffs of key Committee members before finalizing the language of the bill. Members of both teams also reported on the extent of their consultation with "experts" on various components of the bill. Those persons with whom the Select Committee had consulted would also review final drafts of the bill for any further commentary or observations. Plans were made to formulate letters of acknowledgment to the various grassroots advocates who had provided assistance in shaping the bill into a relevant and effective document. The letter would be a personal thank you from Chairman Hall for the suggestions and contributions to the Freedom from Want Act.

The Omnibus antihunger, antipoverty bill had been conceptualized, planned, formulated, discussed, and briefly analyzed from October 1990 through January 1991. In the midst of it all, the Committee's anticipated reauthorization vote occurred on February 6, 1991, after a bit of debate on House Resolution 11, which was introduced by Chairman Hall and all twenty-eight members of the Select Committee. By mid-February, the Select Committee staff was able to finalize its legislative agenda. Many of the items on the legislative agenda for 1991 related to several components of the Freedom from Want Act.

THE BILL AND ITS PROVISIONS

The final framework of the expansive document was fairly comprehensive as well as ambitious. The international component of the bill proposed nine provisions which sought to place the United States in an unequivocal position of leadership in the global effort to reduce hunger over the decade of the nineties. These provisions included: the proposal of a new Convention on Food as a Human Right, the creation of a fund to assist the poorest countries of the Third World who are attempting to move toward democracy; a thirty percent increase in funding for international programs that help children; increases in funding for Women In Development Programs of AID; increased funding for refugee assistance; increased financial assistance to Private Voluntary Organizations; the requirement that agricultural and environmental projects promote renewable natural resources; the authorization of debt relief for certain Third World countries that promote sustainable development; and the involvement of Multilateral Developments and the International Monetary Fund in the alleviation of hunger (U.S. House 1991d).

The domestic provisions of the bill proposed both immediate responses to existing hunger and poverty problems as well as long-term intervention strategies and support to assist low-income persons in achieving economic self-reliance. These provisions included: incremental increases in the WIC program which would expand participation from 51 percent to 100 percent over five to ten years; changes in some regulations of the Food Stamp program which would assist current qualified participants; measures to increase the food purchasing power of low income persons; the development of a survey instrument to assess the extent of food insecurity in communities across the country; the establishment of criteria for communities to meet in order to be designated "hunger-free"; and the creation of demonstration projects to reduce the incidence of low birthweight and infant mortality in high-risk populations. The final draft of the domestic component of the bill also included two provisions which sought to expand self-sufficiency among the poor. One of the provisions was a demonstration project to provide low-income persons the incentive and opportunities to accumulate capital by establishing Individual Development Accounts. The other provision was the promotion of microenterprise opportunities for low-income persons (U.S. House 1991d).

Despite the staff's attempts to complete a sweeping, legal, ethical, humanitarian, comprehensive, and innovative bill by February of 1991, the Freedom from Want Act was not a formal document until April, 1991. Commentaries from members of the advocacy community were essential but debilitating since the complicated range of concerns from key advocates had to be discussed and strongly considered. Addressing the funding for the bill's projects as well as funding for changes in standard poverty program regulations was complex, and several consultations with the Congressional Budget Office were held. Legal aspects of the bill were addressed by the Legislative Counsel office. Several reviews of the language of each section of the bill by specific legislative counselors required weeks of consultation, revising and redrafting of the document. Further, while working on the drafting of the bill, Select Committee staff members were also engaged in addressing ongoing activities, such as organizing regional and local hearings, and preparing the Chairman for domestic and international trips.

On May 8, 1991, Congressman Tony Hall finally introduced the Freedom from Want Act. In his introduction of the bill to the Congress, the Chairman of the Select Committee on Hunger noted that 1991 was the 50th anniversary of President Franklin D. Roosevelt's speech to the Congress, in which he declared that among the four essential human freedoms was freedom from want, which also meant the right to economic security. As originally drafted, the bill consisted of both a domestic title and an international title. Within the boundaries of each title were parts and sections which would be jointly referred to Committees on Education and Labor; Agriculture; Energy and Commerce; Foreign Affairs; Banking, Finance and Urban Affairs; and Ways and Means (U.S. House 1991d).

Under Title I ("Domestic Assistance Programs") of the Freedom from Want Act are eight sections which address "Microenterprise Programs". Among the provisions of this section of the bill were the requirement that microenterprise be included in the training and activities of federal JOBS programs. Another provision of the bill addressed the treatment of resources and income from microenterprise under the Aid to Families with Dependent Children program. This section of the bill also gave the states authority to waive federal AFDC requirements for persons involved in state-approved microenterprise programs. Additionally, there were sections of the bill which addressed rural development grants, community development block grants, microenterprise participation in small business programs; JTPA support of microenterprise activities, and the development of 10 $1 million grants for microenterprise (U.S. House 1991d).

LEGISLATIVE SUPPORT AND ACTIVITIES

By July of 1991, more than one hundred House Members had cosponsored the Freedom from Want Act. More importantly, Representative Perkins, Chairman of the Employment Opportunities Subcommittee of the Education and Labor Committee, included two of the microenterprise training and credit proposals in HR 3033, legislation amending the Job Training Partnership Act. One of the microenterprise amendments added microenterprise to the list of activities authorized to receive JTPA Title II funds. Title II of JTPA addressed training services for economically disadvantaged persons. The amendment also proposed that the Governor adjust standards regarding placement in microenterprises to reflect the time required to establish and develop a stable income from the self-employment venture. The other microenterprise amendment incorporated in the proposed JTPA legislation was the authorization of the Secretary of Labor to award competitive grants (over a five year period) of not more than $500,000 to not more than ten states to implement and enhance community-based microenterprise activities (U.S. House 1991e).

As the bill moved slowly through the Congress, the Select Committee on Hunger moved forward with the new legislative agenda provided by the Freedom From Want Act. On July 18, 1991, a hearing entitled, *"Microeconomic Development Strategies for Rural America"* was held in Washington, D.C. (U.S. House 1991c). The joint committee hearing before the Task Force on Community Development and Natural Resources of the Committee on the Budget, and the Select Committee on Hunger, was chaired by Democratic Congressman Michael Espy, who sat on both committees. While presenting new approaches to increasing economic self-sufficiency among low-income persons in small American communities, the hearing also provided a forum for some members of Congress to express their interest in microenterprise, and to garner interest for their recent legislative initiatives. For example, in his opening statement, Congressman Hall mentioned his introduction of the Freedom From Want Act. He expressed his belief that the bill, which focused on small-scale community development, provided a new way of thinking about the poor and about economic development (U.S. House 1991c, 2-3). Another Representative who promoted a bill was Congresswoman Cardiss Collins, a Democrat from Illinois, who stated, "I am here to discuss H. R. 288, the Act for Microenterprise, which I reintroduced on January 3 of this year, and which now has 32 cosponsors. It's introduction in the Senate in June by Senator Grassley underscores the bipartisan nature of this bill" (U. S. House 1991c, 4). Representative Collins described H.R. 288, the Act for Microenterprise, as a measure which sought to assist Americans attempting to move out of poverty. The proposed legislation also addressed AFDC restrictions by requiring Federal policies to make distinctions between business and personal assets (U.S. House 1991c, 4-5).

Through testimony from members of Congress, the hearing addressed issues related to low-income women. Some Representatives, interested in microenterprise policy, addressed the needs of poor women within specific Congressional districts. Representative Collins illustrated the importance of microenterprise to low-income women by presenting an example of a young woman in Chicago who had a sound business idea which would help the people in her community but was hindered by federal welfare restrictions. The Congresswoman's example focused on the stifled capabilities of poor women, and the oppressive nature of welfare policies (U.S. House 1991c, 4-7). Another reference to low-income women and microenterprise was presented at the hearing by Congressman Espy, who spoke of a young woman in his Mississippi district. Although this former welfare recipient had established a potentially successful car detailing business, at the time, she was no longer eligible for the medical benefits provided by Medicaid. The Congressman reported that because there was no transition mechanism for public assistance recipients who start microenterprises, many low-income women were reluctant to risk losing the few benefits available to them (U.S. House 1991c, 6).

Yet another testimony focusing on the importance of microenterprise to low-income women was that of Representative Nancy Pelosi, a Democrat from California, who argued that microenterprise is a new way for some women to escape poverty. Citing some examples of microenterprise programs from her district in San Francisco, Representative Pelosi described the Women's Initiative for Self Employment (WISE), which enables low-income women to earn adequate incomes through self-employment, while at the same time acknowledging women's particular family and work responsibilities. Representative Pelosi called upon the Government to support organizations which provide loans, grants and technical assistance to low-income women (U.S. House 1991c, 112-116).

Following the hearing on microenterprise and rural America, the Select Committee held two other related hearings. One hearing, entitled *"New Perspectives on Urban Poverty and Microenterprise Development"* was held in Washington, D.C. on July 25, 1991. Included in this hearing were prepared statements from the U.S. Conference of Mayors and two university professors, all of whom addressed the issue of urban poverty in America (U.S. House 1991b). The other related hearing was entitled, *"New Strategies for Alleviating Poverty: Building Hope by Building Assets"*, and was held on October 9, 1991 (U.S. House 1991a). Like the previous hearing, this hearing supported the provisions of the Freedom from Want Act.

Although hearings provided a well-organized arena for the promotion of microenterprise and the Freedom from Want Act, the Select Committee also publicized its legislative initiatives through news releases in the Washington Post and other national newspapers. Shortly after the bill's introduction, an article by columnist William Raspberry on June 28, 1991, recounted the plight of poor entrepreneurs and some provisions of the emerging legislation introduced by Tony Hall. The Select Committee also informed advocacy groups of its activities through a monthly news release called *"The Hunger Report"*. In a lead article entitled, *"Welfare Penalizes Entrepreneurs"*, the report described two women who were attempting to leave welfare and enter the world of self-employment. However, welfare restrictions on assets and income could stifle their efforts to become self-sufficient. The article described the provisions of the Freedom from Want Act which would allow these women the opportunity to develop businesses (U.S. House 1992).

Despite its record of diligently addressing issues related to hunger and poverty, the Select Committee on Hunger remained under the harsh scrutiny of the Congress. Some members of powerful standing committees felt that the work done by the staff of the Select Committee on Hunger could be carried out more efficiently within the jurisdiction of such committees as Education and Labor. The Select Committee on Hunger staff had always operated under the threat of elimination, and in early 1993, it was clear that the Committee's demise would soon become a reality. On March 31, 1993, the Select Committee on Hunger became a historical entity of the United States House of Representatives. Its traditions would be reshaped into the Congressional Hunger Center and the Congressional Hunger Caucus, both of which would be chaired by Congressman Tony Hall. Like the Select Committee on Hunger, the Freedom from Want Act also passed into the annals of Congressional history. As of September 1994, very little action had been taken on the microenterprise components of this bill. Microenterprise development for low-income women continues to be an extraordinarily challenging experience, and welfare reform continues to focus on punitive rather than positive measures.

CONCLUSION

The Freedom from Want Act became the legislative vehicle which defined the Select Committee's activities in the 102nd Congress. In particular, the Select Committee's focus on microenterprise provided a new level of legislative expertise for the Committee which the staff hoped would support its reauthorization in years to come. Historically, the Select Committee's initial interest in microenterprise was demonstrated by hearings and reports on microenterprise in economically underdeveloped countries. In cooperation with international organizations such as AID, members of Congress held hearings and introduced legislation promoting international microenterprise initiatives.

Evolving from these activities was the Select Committee's inevitable interest in domestic microenterprise. When the need for a domestic focus on microenterprise came to the Committee's attention, the Select Committee issued its first report addressing small business development for the poor. However, it was not until the development of the domestic microenterprise portion of the Freedom from Want Act that the Committee assumed a proactive stance on microenterprise for low income persons in the United States. The focus on domestic microenterprise connected the eradication of poverty to economic empowerment and served the Committee politically as well.

Among the political factors influencing the Select Committee's development of the Freedom from Want Act was Congressman Tony Hall's need for an issue which would firmly establish him as the rightful chairman of the Select Committee on Hunger. The proposal and introduction of a comprehensive, highly visible omnibus bill during the Select Committee's transition period was an effective strategy to overshadow the legacy of the very popular Congressman, Mickey Leland. Another political factor was the "anti-encumbancy fever" of voters which was apparent in the 1990 Congressional elections. Although Tony Hall's Congressional seat had remained unchallenged for several years, there was perhaps some anticipation of a challenger in 1992. Another factor influencing the development of the Freedom from Want Act (and particularly the development of microenterprise) was a call for welfare reform by the voters and the Congress. By focusing on the idea of self-sufficiency, the Congressman could distance himself from the liberal advocacy stance previously assumed by the Select Committee on Hunger.

The historical and political factors which influenced the development of policy on microenterprise also connected the Select Committee on Hunger to the economic lives of low income women. Throughout the testimony of international and domestic hearings were examples of women's involvement in self-generated economic activities. Although the language of the bill did not include specific references to women or women's microenterprise initiatives, Select Committee hearing reports and staff reports strongly suggest that the majority of low income entrepreneurs are women. Yet, as advocates and members of Congress indicate, support for microenterprise includes increasing the number of projects available in states and eliminating restrictive welfare regulations. These regulations primarily affect poor women and their children. Hence, the introduction of the Freedom from Want Act was one step toward acknowledging women as active participants in their own economic empowerment, and reinforcing the critical interweaving of gender, class, economics and policy.

VI

Radical Political Economy:
Analysis of Major Concepts

*"Poverty is not an unfortunate accident, a residue, an indication that
the great American mobility machine missed a minority of the people.
On the contrary, always it has been a necessary result of America's
distinctive political economy."*

-Michael Katz, *The Undeserving Poor*

THE POLITICAL ECONOMY OF THE NEW
PARADIGM

Microenterprise, or very small business ownership by low
income persons, was one aspect of the Bush Administration's New
Paradigm. This economic development idea symbolized an attempt by
President Bush and other Republican leaders to revitalize a neglected
and dreary domestic agenda. In anticipation of the 1992 election,
President Bush's policy planners formulated ideas on empowerment
that would address the ills of low income America,oterincluding
suggestions for reforms in health, housing and education, welfare and
small enterprise. Although Bush's strategies for gaining the confidence
of the American voter failed, the New Paradigm did stimulate some
bipartisan activities on domestic policy in the United States Congress.
One of several Congressional responses to the New Paradigm was the
formulation of the Freedom from Want Act by the House Select
Committee on Hunger.

It is very evident from the Select Committee's hearing reports
that the Committee's international task force had included
microenterprise initiatives in its legislative agenda. It is also evident
that the Select Committee's interest in domestic microenterprise
assistance programs was stimulated by these early international policy
activities. However, it is also important to understand that much of the
focus on microenterprise by the Select Committee on Hunger and other
Congressional bodies was stimulated by the political necessity to
respond to President Bush's New Paradigm concepts. Both
Republicans and Democrats, liberal and conservatives, debated the
effectiveness of the New Paradigm concepts and attempted to

formulate their own definitions of reform and empowerment.

From the perspective of political economy analysis, the Bush Administration and the New Paradigm represented the larger system, a powerful structure which stimulated many responses in the form of political rhetoric and national policies by both Republicans and Democrats. The United States Congress, with its ability to formulate policy on the economic lives of the poor, is also a part of the power structure. The policies generated by the Congress may appear to be productive and effective in addressing the problems of the poor (who are embedded within the larger system). However, the policy formulation process does not eliminate gender and class hierarchies which are at the core of economic discrimination. Further, the policy formulation process, because it primarily involves those who are in power, continues to reinforce the asymmetrical relationship that exists between policymakers and the poor.

In order to determine some of the political and economic implications of the activities of the larger system, major concepts and themes of this book will be discussed. Included in this discussion are some comments on the relevancy of this study to the discipline of anthropology.

THE ROLE OF POLICY

In order to understand the relationship between microenterprise and policy, I observed the policy formulation process of the Select Committee on Hunger as it occurred in 1991. One of the most fascinating aspects of the Select Committee's work at that time was the formulation of the Freedom From Want Act, an omnibus bill which proposed to advance innovative economic options for the poor. Earlier in the Committee's history, the international task force had investigated the viability of credit assistance to the poor by traveling to economically disadvantaged countries, holding joint hearings on microenterprise assistance, and issuing reports on microenterprise that included policy recommendations. One result of these early international activities in 1986 and 1987, was the development of interest in the issue of domestic microenterprise. The Select Committee's 1987 report entitled, *"Access and Availability of Credit to the Poor in Developing Countries and in the United States"* illustrated a heightened awareness of the need for credit assistance and microenterprise initiatives in America's low income communities. From this report and subsequent reports, the Select Committee's domestic task force began to focus on microenterprise as a possible strategy for fighting poverty and hunger. In 1991, amid drastically declining public trust of Congress, growing public resentment of America's social service system, Republican rhetoric packaged in the New Paradigm, and the need to revive the Select Committee's legislative agenda, ideas for the Freedom From Want Act gradually emerged and evolved.

House Resolution 2258, also known as The Freedom From Want Act, was a comprehensive bill which included legislative language on both international and domestic programs. The actual document, presented to the 102nd Congress on May 8, 1991, was 177 pages of Committee findings, amendments, and mandates on hunger-related programs. By far, the most substantive component of the bill was that part of the document which addressed domestic microenterprise initiatives. One provision of the microenterprise section of the bill included the addition of microenterprise activities as part of the federal JOBS program. Another provision gave states the authority to waive federal AFDC requirements for persons enrolled in state-approved microenterprise assistance programs. The microenterprise sections of the bill also addressed development grants for microenterprise in rural communities, Community Development Block Grants, JTPA support of microenterprise and the development of ten $1 million grants for microenterprise initiatives across the United States.

What can anthropologists learn from the Select Committee's policy formulation process on microenterprise? One of the first things that should be understood is the role of that group of people, generically known as "the staff", who are indeed the foundation of policymaking. Despite the media's focus on Washington's celebrities and scandals, the Congress consists primarily of average people who work for the government. Many staff members stumble into Congressional policy work on the way to other careers. People remain in Washington either because they are captured by the deceptive notion that the Congress is the center of the universe, or because they honestly feel that they have something to contribute. Astute or shrewd staff people learn very quickly how to function with very limited direction or support. The staff persons who gain financially (through yearly raises and bonuses) are those who prove themselves to be loyal, supportive, and hard-working. Staff members can distinguish themselves by developing expertise on various issues so that their Member of Congress can always present intelligent or politically astute views to the American public. Through hearings, press conferences, and other publicized events, Members of Congress appear informed and resolute on the issues of the day. Yet, behind the bright lights of the daily photo opportunities, are the people who write speeches, and make schedules, telephone calls, connections, and policy. If it is true that anthropologists must "use the knowledge, skills and perspective of their discipline to help solve human problems and facilitate change" (Chambers 1985, 8), then it is important that anthropologists observe and describe the culture of Congressional staff members and the effect of this culture on the policy process.

        Anthropologists must also understand the political motivations that influence the development of policy. In the United States Congress, attaching oneself to a socially relevant or media-engaged issue is synonymous with political survival. This was no less true for Chairman Hall, who in 1991 was still attempting to distance the Select Committee on Hunger from the legacy of Mickey Leland. Although Congressman Hall was a twelve-year veteran of the House of Representatives, and fairly popular in his Dayton District, he was not a nationally recognized figure. Further, before his appointment to the Chair, the Congressman had never introduced any significant legislation. Thus, Chairman Hall's introduction of a highly visible, well-publicized omnibus bill which promoted innovative options for the poor, was indeed strongly connected with the need to revive and preserve a political career.

        Another factor in policy formulation that anthropologists must understand is that most policies are not necessarily innovative. Policies should arise out of a need to eliminate or alleviate human social problems. However, since the shaping of a poverty-related bill involves much political compromise and economic considerations, there is little room for bold, creative ideas which would truly serve the masses. Most of the microenterprise provisions of the Freedom From Want Act, (although more substantive than other parts of the bill) were not innovative because they did not challenge the hierarchical system that thrives on and contributes to poverty and hunger. For example, the provisions did not address banking institutions, nor did the provisions address the role that lending institutions could play in the success of microenterprise. Also, the provisions did not address some of the most effective aspects of a successful microenterprise program such as solidarity or peer group lending. Further, the provisions did not go far enough in dismantling restrictive welfare regulations. Thus, the microenterprise provisions of the Freedom From Want Act, which included demonstration projects and the attachment of microenterprise to standard federal social service programs, did nothing innovative, bold, or challenging for the concept of microenterprise. Despite this, the policies could prove to be effective in increasing microenterprise programs (particularly in rural areas) and in establishing a foundation for future innovative polices on microenterprise.

Another aspect of policy that anthropologists can learn from this research is the significance of collaboration in the development of policy. Historically, the Select Committee on Hunger had always recognized the need to work in coalition with grassroots organizations. The sixty-five national grassroots organizations composing the Coalition for the Select Committee on Hunger played a key role in influencing the initial authorization of the Committee. In 1991, the Committee's extensive connections with nongovernmental bodies was no less apparent during the formulation of the Freedom From Want Act. Every aspect of the microenterprise portion of the bill was reviewed by several grassroots advocates, including consultants from the Corporation for Enterprise Development (CfED). In fact, prior to the initial drafting of the bill, staff members from CfED met with the domestic task force in order to clarify some issues related to microenterprise. The connection and collaboration with advocacy organizations served not only to keep the Select Committee on Hunger aware of the needs of poor Americans, but also, until 1993, this collaboration served to keep the Committee alive in the House of Representatives.

WOMEN'S SELF-GENERATED ECONOMIC STRATEGIES

This book has also explored and described some issues germane to low income women's self-generated economic strategies. Four basic points were presented for consideration. First was the assertion that a significant number of women welfare recipients seek ways of disengaging themselves from the social service system. The plausibility of this point was based upon literature describing entrepreneurial assistance programs for poor women and reports from joint Congressional Committee hearings on microenterprise. The literature and the reports suggest that a considerable proportion of potential microentrepreneurs are low income women who receive federally subsidized cash benefits, food assistance, health care, child care or housing. Secondly was the argument that the development of very small businesses offers low income women the opportunities to become productively employed, make economic choices that are relevant to their lives, and to eventually become economically empowered. Thirdly was the assertion that there are a number of organizations and projects which are assisting these women. Examples were presented of several domestic microenterprise projects that are working to meet the entrepreneurial needs of those with limited economic resources, including public assistance recipients. Finally, there was the argument that low income women face many social, political and bureaucratic barriers in their attempts to become self-sufficient through business ownership. Aside from the prejudicial rules of banking institutions, there are also restrictive regulations embedded within the welfare system which impede or prevent the initiation or sustaining of microenterprises for poor women. These regulations are disguised as policies that protect the capitalist system, the economy, and tax payers against fraud or abuse. Although protective in intent, these policies are punitive in practice, and prevent welfare recipients from accumulating working capital for potential businesses. Further, these welfare regulations have an impact on microenterprise assistance projects due to the complex, bureaucratic waiver writing process which is necessary in order for the project participants to begin their businesses. Consideration of these ideas on women's self-generated economic activities led to the development of some divergent yet complimentary perspectives on the concept of microenterprise.

PERSPECTIVES ON MICROENTERPRISE

The concept of microenterprise was introduced as an economic development tool. As such, microenterprise could conceivably offer one potential solution to women's poverty and hunger. Because the concept of microenterprise is cultural, complex, and multidimensional, it was necessary to formulate definitions and understand how this concept intersects with other related cultural constructs such as mutual aid societies, the informal economy, work, and economic development. It was also important to illustrate some parallels between microenterprise and the work that women do. Thus, within the framework of this book, microenterprise was presented from several perspectives.

One perspective equated microenterprise with entrepreneurship. Associating low income women's economic strategies with entrepreneurship challenges conventional economic thought about the contributions of the poor. Yet, despite the absence of women from traditional, theories of entrepreneurship, many of the characteristics associated with entrepreneurs (innovativeness, risk-taking, assertiveness, and decision-making) are apparent in women's microenterprise development. The most constructive way of connecting microenterprise to entrepreneurship is by considering both concepts within local contexts. When the definition of entrepreneurship is broadened to address gender and class issues, the mystique of business ownership is eliminated, and the work that women microentrepreneurs do can be recognized as socially and culturally valuable as well as economically valid. Further, associating the two concepts as complimentary renders power to the concept of microenterprise in that entrepreneurship implies initiative, innovation, and the potential for success.

Another perspective on microenterprise was presented in the form of the microenterprise assistance project. International and domestic programs offer a range of services to participants including business training, skill building, access to the ideas of other microentrepreneurs and various forms of credit assistance. From this perspective, microenterprise can be seen as part of the economic development planning for a particular community. Microenterprise assistance programs themselves become entrepreneurial in that the directors and trainers must invent ways to insure that the projects will survive. Project survival depends on such factors as adequate funding, active participation by the target population, successful business starts by participants, and the administrators' ability to surmount certain policy obstacles. Viewing microenterprise within the context of the assistance project places emphasis on the state and does not focus enough on the participants. This perspective also diminishes the power of the concept because many projects operate within the framework of social service agencies. As such, potential microentrepreneurs are viewed as recipients or the objects of microenterprise rather than the reason for the development or success of the projects.

Microenterprise was also presented and explored as a policy issue. Clearly, a symbiotic relationship exists between a successful microenterprise project and the generation of sound, supportive policies at the state and federal levels. At the state level, policies contribute to the initiation or expansion of microenterprise within certain communities. For example, when the state of Maryland agreed to establish Business Owners Start-Up Services (BOSS) as an economic development demonstration project, microenterprise became one of several options in the state's work and training initiatives. Policies on the design and implementation of the project had to be created. Moreover, some federal policies that interfered with the development of individual microenterprises had to be modified. One example of such modification is the application process for the waiving of selected federal welfare regulations. In order for the BOSS participants to continue to receive social service support while establishing businesses, certain welfare policies had to be amended temporarily through the waiver process. Another example of policy modification is evident in the number of participants involved in informal businesses. In order to assist participants who may have business experience through informal economic activities, certain social service policies restricting "underground businesses" had to be ignored by the BOSS director and trainers. Thus, the state's responsibilities in the development of microenterprise were assumed primarily by the director and trainers of BOSS, who worked within the boundaries as well as on the fringes of social service policy. At the federal level, microenterprise was presented as an issue with which policymakers were gradually becoming familiar. Various members of Congress and their staffs were attempting to determine the most practical and judicious way of supporting microenterprise. In order to formulate adequate policies on microenterprise, federal policymakers consulted experts on microenterprise in various states and attempted to draft legislation based on information gleaned from these observations and consultations.

Microenterprise was also presented as a political vehicle for the Chairman of the Select Committee on Hunger. Indeed, microenterprise became the major issue around which the Freedom from Want Act was formulated. Sensing the political expediency of distancing himself from so called liberal values (with which the Select Committee's first Chairman had been very comfortable), Congressman Hall requested the formulation of an omnibus bill which would emphasize work and taxable assets rather than dependency and benefits for the poor. Microenterprise served as least two political purposes for Representative Hall and the Select Committee on Hunger. First, microenterprise offered a response to what politicians perceived as the public's demand for welfare reform. In Congressional communications to constituents, microenterprise was presented not only as a strategy for employing welfare recipients but also as a method of reducing AFDC and other social service costs. Secondly, involvement in microenterprise showed that the Select Committee could be proactive in its approach to poverty issues. Historically, the Select Committee had been a Congressional body which responded to imminent crises quickly and effectively with palliative legislation.

However, developing policy on microenterprise appeared to be a way of planning for economic needs before the emergence of crises. Also, the development of some long term ideas on microenterprise policy gave the appearance of the Select Committee as "visionary" in its approach to poverty.

Microenterprise was explored as an independent, self-generated strategy for economic survival, particularly for low income women. This view of microenterprise speaks to the cultural phenomenon of class struggle and the drive to accumulate capital. In order to launch small businesses or legitimize their ongoing informal businesses, some low income women enroll in microenterprise assistance projects. While benefiting from the projects, these women are also challenging a system whose policies dictate that they remain in poverty. The struggle with the system begins when the welfare recipients approach their social service case managers for referrals to the microenterprise program. Reports from participants and trainers at Business Owners Start up Services in Maryland indicate that approvals or denials of referrals from case managers depend on arbitrary, subjective opinions about the welfare recipient's character, intelligence, or ability.

The perspective of microenterprise as an economic survival strategy for women also illuminates the fact that in America, women are divided by class issues. This division is particularly evident in the policies of lending institutions. That is, women who have economic resources through support from spouses, are more likely to be considered responsible and respectable. Therefore, these women are more likely to have access to the resources of lending institutions. Also, middle class women are more likely to have access to business training that is not connected to social service agencies. Microenterprise training projects are class-specific in that the participants are primarily women whose income is at or below the poverty line. Another class issue that divides women is that for women with resources, business development may arise because of a need to express creativity, to supplement the income of a spouse, or to provide extra resources for the family. While poor women may also seek to supplement an income or express creative talents, typically, their business ideas arise out of economic necessity. Further, unlike middle-class women, poor women (many of whom are single mothers) have no significant income with which to support their families while developing their businesses. This factor either prolongs a women's dependency on public assistance or discourages women from initiating businesses.

While the division of women by class is evident in those processes that characterize microenterprise, we can also see how the concept serves to unite self-employed women. No matter how small the enterprise, women's self-employment speaks to the changing nature of women's work and home lives. For all women business owners, their roles in business development are distinguishable from their traditional roles as primary caretakers of households. The idea of business ownership by women challenges traditional cultural beliefs about women's abilities to make choices and behave autonomously in their work lives. Yet, for many women (particularly those who are poor), business development is an economic activity that occurs in conjunction with their household and child care responsibilities. However, women's participation in microenterprise represents their ability to take risks, their willingness to challenge institutionalized racism, classism, and sexism, and their awareness of the necessity of economic empowerment.

PERSPECTIVES ON THIRD WORLD MODELS

One of the most predominant themes throughout this research is the significance of certain economic development paradigms imported from non-Western nations. The substantive value of Third World microenterprise activities was very apparent in the hearing records of the international task force of the Select Committee on Hunger. The Select Committee's initial interest in microenterprise focused on the policies of international and multilateral funding agencies. In 1986 and 1987 the Select Committee held hearings and issued reports on the necessity of credit assistance and microenterprise to the poor in countries such as Bangladesh, with its staggering numbers of women living in dire poverty. Information from the hearings and reports provided the basis for understanding some critical features of microenterprise programs. As the Select Committee's legislative agenda evolved and as more information on microenterprise was obtained, a domestic focus on microenterprise was evident in hearings and committee reports. Some of the most successful and well-publicized microenterprise assistance programs in the United States are based on models from poor countries. These models speak not only to economic empowerment, but also to the economic and political awareness of the poor. For example, the Progresso program in Peru, the Association for the Development of Microenterprises in the Dominican Republic and the Program of

Partnership for Productivity in Kenya are described as projects which have focused specifically on women's economic development by emphasizing informality, respect for traditions, solidarity group lending, and credit to the poorest of the poor. Moreover, the Self-Employed Women's Association (SEWA) in India, the SEWA Bank and the Grameen Bank in Bangladesh are shown to have originated from the development of social/political consciousness as well as liberation struggles. As such, the SEWA Bank instituted an advocacy approach to lending, and eliminated some of the formal constraints of the banking system. The practices of the Grameen Bank helped to organize and mobilize the poor, and assist them in moving toward accumulation of capital and assets. These international microenterprise assistance projects and credit institutions have served as models for the Women's Self-Employment Project in Chicago, Illinois and the Women's Economic Development Corporation in St. Paul, Minnesota.

What can anthropologists, advocates, and policymakers learn from microenterprise initiatives in less wealthy countries? One principle that could be gleaned is that programs for the poor, and particularly for poor women, do not have to focus on the poor only as recipients. Rather, programs for the poor can consider the potential economic contributions of microentrepreneurs and provide support which will gradually lead to economic stability. This means respecting people's business ideas, eliminating complex bureaucratic policies, realizing the long term nature of small business support, and distancing microenterprise assistance projects from the social service framework. When economically disadvantaged women are seen only as recipients of social services, their capacity to view themselves as independent persons is diminished. However, when economic endeavors are acknowledged and supported, poor women can see themselves as potential contributors to the economy.

Another insight that could be gained from Third World models of microenterprise is that great numbers of poor people know how to generate economies and indeed carry out these strategies informally. Anthropologists (including Berger 1989; Bunster 1985; Moore 1988; Peattie 1987; and Ehlers 1990) have analyzed and documented these kinds of economic activities. Perhaps some awareness of poor people's abilities by policymakers, would compel them to reconsider the necessity and validity of the informal economy in the development of microenterprises. Hoke (1990) indicates that informal businesses may be more important to the economy than official figures suggest. These businesses, which are unrecorded for various reasons, may represent $500 billion annually -- excluding criminal activity (Hoke 1990:13). Providing the financial support and technical training for informal business owners allows them to legitimize their businesses and contribute to the national economy. Related to this is the idea that American policymakers may have to modify their views on capitalism and consider the possibility that capitalism could work more effectively if more emphasis is placed on small scale enterprises.

Another lesson that can be learned from analyzing microenterprise activities in poor countries is that microenterprise should be thought of as a movement. In the tradition of other poor people's movements, the Grameen Bank, and the Self-Employed Women's Association raised poor people's consciouses and supported them in demanding their right to credit. Advocates for microenterprise development in the United States should consider educating the general public about the potential contributions of microentrepreneurs. Advocates should also emphasize the particular needs of microentrepreneurs to state and federal policymakers. Further, microentrepreneurs should be encouraged to organize, lobby policymakers (through letters and meetings), and think of their business endeavors as community development initiatives.

Another lesson that can be learned from Third World models of microenterprise is that, although every aspect of our economic system should be questioned and critically analyzed, we should particularly question the concept of collateral and the inherent sexist, racist, and classist implications of this concept. In his research which led to the growth of the Grameen Bank system, Dr. Mohammed Yunus observed how the concept of collateral serves to increase the assets of the wealthy and prevent the poor from progressing economically. In the United States, collateral is a mechanism used by lending institutions to determine the credibility and financial stability of potential loan recipients. Only those loan applicants who possess certain financial resources are considered for loans. Lending institutions feel justified in establishing criteria based on collateral because there is some assurance that loans will be repaid. However, collateral is also a way of automatically disqualifying poor persons from the loan application process. Banks could be a primary lending source for microenterprises, which generally require relatively small amounts of start-up capital. Therefore, it is important to analyze policies on collateral, and consider ways in which microenterprise assistance programs can encourage banks to support low income women entrepreneurs.

Finally, one of the most essential lessons that can be learned from Third World models of microenterprise is the value of ideas like reciprocity, trust, and welfare of the group. The critical nature of these concepts to the perpetuation of culture is very evident in the anthropological literature on mutual aid societies and rotating credit associations. In Africa, South America, Asia, and the Caribbean, microenterprise assistance projects require participants to form solidarity groups or loan circles. While the most obvious goal of membership is individual loan acquisition, the entire group is accountable for the financial behavior of each member. Thus, default or mismanagement of a loan by one member of the group results in penalty for all members of the group. Similarly, the financial success of individual group members contributes to the success of the entire group. For low income women in the United States, an emphasis on group support, sharing of resources, and mutual trust would stimulate increased participation in microenterprise. The solidarity group concept could also contribute to higher success rates among women microentrepreneurs by providing an element of social support which may be absent in formal assistance programs.

PERSPECTIVES ON WOMEN AND THE STATE

Another very apparent theme evolving from this research is that of the relationship of poor women to the state. In fact, at the core of this research are concerns about the nature of the relationship between women and the state, as well as the nature of women's poverty. As part of my examination of the policy process I attempted to determine the connection between the Select Committee on Hunger and the lives of poor women. I determined that from its inception, the Select Committee on Hunger established itself as an advocate for the welfare of poor women. This was particularly evident in the Committee's legislative initiatives with AFDC, Food Stamps, and WIC. In hearings and reports, the Select Committee showed unequivocal support for those programs which assist poor women and their children. While this Congressional support was vital, it also served to perpetuate the idea of women as dependents. Thus, the maternal roles of women and the idea of women as objects of the social service system were linked and reinforced. However, the issue of microenterprise offered a new perspective on the potential and abilities of low income women. Much of the literature consulted by Select Committee staff members described microenterprise assistance programs for women. Both internationally and domestically, most of the participants in microenterprise assistance programs are low income women who seek to create jobs and generate self-supporting incomes. Yet, in its formulation of the Freedom From Want Act, the Select Committee made no specific references to women as a unique constituency. This omission speaks to a continued Congressional reluctance to recognize the changing nature of women's lives as well as women's needs for economic choices. It is very interesting to note that in discussions of welfare reform, policymakers and others readily identify "welfare mothers" as the most problematic participants in America's welfare system. Yet in policies on microenterprise, women as a specific constituency are not distinguished. Despite the formulation of legislation on domestic microenterprise, women microentrepreneurs' needs for technological training, child care, health care, sustained financial support, asset-building mechanisms, and other support systems remain invisible.

RECOMMENDATIONS

An anthropological study of this kind should not only describe and document issues related to contemporary problems, but should also offer some recommendations for future anthropological studies. One recommendation is that more ethnographic studies of the Congressional policy environment be conducted by anthropologists. Ethnographic research describing the policy process as well as the impact of political and social factors on policy will contribute to the development of anthropology as a policy science. During the time I spent on Capitol Hill, I met scholars from various disciplines, including political science, psychology, and history. All of these people were involved in understanding the policy process and interpreting that process from the perspective of their respective disciplines. As the only anthropologist among other Congressional fellows, I sensed the need for more anthropological investigation of the culture of the policy environment. Hence, I recommend more anthropological research on Congressional Committees and Congressional staff offices.

Aside from the need to understand the policy environment, there is also a continuing need for anthropologists to become more involved in contemporary social problems. Hence, I recommend more anthropological analyses of problems related to domestic poverty and economic development. As social scientists who have traditionally focused on the problems and activities of people in other countries, American anthropologists have neglected many of the very serious problems facing people in this country. There is a particular need for anthropologists to focus attention on the problems of gender, class, and ethnicity in urban and rural America. Involvement in domestic issues by anthropological scholars can contribute to a relevant, action-oriented anthropology.

There should also be more anthropological studies on microenterprise and domestic microenterprise assistance projects. Most of the anthropological literature on self-generated economic activities consists of studies on the informal economy and petty commerce among people in other countries. The Women in Development literature also contributes to anthropological knowledge on economic strategies of poor people. However, there are no anthropological studies of microenterprise assistance projects in the United States, nor are there anthropological studies of the participants in these projects. Anthropologists can contribute to the success of these projects by collecting qualitative data that could assist in program evaluation. Anthropologists can also collect qualitative data on the project participants that would contribute to the development of culturally relevant microenterprise assistance programs. Through involvement in domestic social policy, urban and rural poverty issues, and economic development planning, anthropologists can contribute to the growth of the discipline. Anthropologists can also contribute to constructive social change by finding solutions for those who live in poverty in America.

A FEMINIST ANTHROPOLOGIST'S CONCLUDING THOUGHTS ON WOMEN'S MICROENTERPRISE

Through the prism of radical political economy, I have investigated some of the circumstances involved in policy formulation on microenterprise. As such, I have analyzed the various cultural uses of policy, including those which perpetuate a powerful capitalist system. In my descriptions of policy formulation, I have also looked at the constraints of policy on the economic lives of low income women. Because political economy speaks to those issues involved in class struggle, I have analyzed low income women as an oppressed group, their relationship to the state, and their attempts to develop microenterprises.

Many questions remain concerning low income women and the development of sound and relevant policy on microenterprise. These questions are all embedded within the concept of women and the state. Specifically, what can be done to change state policies that are more an expression of economically advantaged male interests than those interests of impoverished women? What can be done to change the detrimental impact of certain governmental policies on low income women? In order to address these questions it is very important to realize that policies reflect assumptions about the intersection of gender, class, economics, and power. Moore acknowledges the crucial link between women's status and state policies, and concludes, "...it is quite clear that state policies affect the social position of women, and that through economic, political and legal practices they determine how much control women have over their lives" (Moore 1988, 128). Katz expands upon Moore's observation by commenting on the intersection of poverty, gender and the state, "Women's poverty is a political as well as economic issue, for it links women, the state and the meaning of citizenship" (Katz 1989, 75).

One particular question remains concerning the viability of women's microenterprise within the traditional, patriarchal, and powerful capitalist structure. Is microenterprise a workable strategy for the economic empowerment of low income women? There may be many answers to this question depending upon the context in which it is posed. However, when asking this question we must consider the political environment of 1994 which is very resistant to change not only on views concerning women and welfare, but also on opinions about poor women's rights to make choices about business ownership. Thus, if the assumptions which inform policy continue to view women only in terms of their roles as exploitative dependents, or in terms of their roles in maintaining two-parent, one-wage earner families, policies will continue to restrict women's economic development and autonomy. Further these policies will not reflect the particular economic needs of low income women microentrepreneurs, and microenterprise will be a viable options for a very limited number of people. However, if all women are seen as "social actors who are involved in social strategies, with both short- and long-term aims" (Moore 1988, 134), and if poor women are viewed as capable, creative contributors to economic development, then policies will be formulated to reflect these images. Further, if successful women microentrepreneurs can encourage other women to mobilize and organize themselves into advocates for microenterprise development, policymakers will have to respond to women as an empowered constituency by formulating relevant and substantive policies. It is only through these policies that microenterprise can become a revolutionary remedy for some of the economic ills of a powerful but inherently unequal capitalist society.

Bibliography

Amott, Teresa L., and Julie A. Matthaei. *Race Gender and Work: A Multicultural Economic History of Women in the United States.* Boston: South End Press, 1991.

Arizpe, Lourdes. "Women in the Informal Sector: the Case of Mexico City." In *Women and National Development: The Complexities of Change*, edited by Wellesley Editorial Committee, 25-37. Chicago: University of Chicago Press, 1977.

Balkin, Steven. *Self-Employment for Low Income People: A Report to the National Commission on Jobs and Small Business.* Springfield, VA: National Technical Information Service, 1986.

Balkin, Steven. *Self-Employment for Low Income People.* New York: Praeger Press, 1989.

Balkin, Steven. "Self-Employment Training Programs for the Poor." *Journal of Small Business Strategy* 1 (1990): 47-56.

Barlow, Kathleen. "The Role of Women in Intertribal Trade Among the Murik of Papua New Guinea." In *Research in Economic Anthropology*, edited by Barry L. Isaac, 95-122. Greenwich, Connecticut: JAI Press, 1985.

Barone, Michael, and Grant Ujifusa. *The Almanac of American Politics 1990.* Washington, D.C.: Times Mirror Press, 1989.

Barrett, Richard A. *Culture and Conduct.* Belmont, California: Wadsworth Publishing Co., 1984.

Becker, E. H. "Self-Employed Workers: An Update to 1983." *Monthly Labor Review* (1984): 14 -18.

Berger, Marguerite. Introduction to *Women's Ventures: Assistance to the Informal Sector in Latin America*, edited by Marguerite Berger and Mayra Buvinic, 1-18. Connecticut: Kumarian Press, 1989.

Bunster, Ximena, and Elsa M. Chaney. *Sellers and Servants: Women Working in Lima, Peru.* New York: Praeger, 1985.

Chambers, Erve. *Applied Anthropology A Practical Guide.* New Jersey: Prentice-Hall, Inc., 1985.

Casson, M. *The Entrepreneur: An Economic Theory.* New Jersey: Barnes and Noble Books, 1982.

Clammer, John. *Anthropology and Political Economy.* New York: St. Martin's Press, 1985.

Crane, Julia, and Michael Angrosino. *Field Projects in Anthropology.* New Jersey: General Learning Press, 1974.

Crawford, Lynda V. E. "Mickey Leland: A Hunger Fighter Who Gave His Life." *Seeds* (1989): 18-24.

Denzin, Norman. *The Research Act.* New York: McGraw Hill, 1989.

Dickerson-Putman, Jeanette. 'Women's Contribution to the Domestic and National Economy of Papua New Guinea." In *Research in Economic Anthropology,* edited by Barry L. Isaac, 201-222. Connecticut: JAI Press, 1988.

Donovan, Josephine. *Feminist Theory: The Intellectual Traditions of American Feminism.* New York: Ungar, 1987.

Eddy, Elizabeth, and William Partridge, ed. *Applied Anthropology in America.* New York: Columbia University Press, 1990.

Ehlers, Tracy Bachrach. *Silent Looms: Women and Production in a Guatemalan Town.* San Francisco: Westview Press, 1990.

Feit, Rona. "The U.S. Experience: Self-Employment Programs for the Disadvantaged." In *The Self-Employment Strategy: Gaining Momentum,* edited by the Self-Employment Development Initiative and the Corporation for Enterprise Development, 31-41. Washington, D.C.: CfED, 1990.

Feit, Rona, and Sheela Rani Das. "Wading Through the Waivers: Enabling Self-Employment for Welfare Entrepreneurs." *Entrepreneurial Economy Review* (1990): 3-9.

Friedman, Robert. "Expanding the Vision of the Entrepreneurial Economy." *Entrepreneurial Economy* 4 (1987): 2-3.

Geertz, Clifford. *Interpretation of Cultures.* New York: Basic Books, 1973.

Gellatly, Lynne. *Women's Self-Employment Project: An Overview.* Report on file. Chicago, Illinois: Women, Self-Employment Project, 1990.

Gelpi, Barbara, Nancy Hartsock, C. Novak, and M. Strober, ed. *Women and Poverty.* Chicago: Univerity of Chicago Press, 1986.

Glastris, Paul. "Inner-City Lending: Hits and Misses." *U.S. News and World Report* (1993): 65.

Gould, Sara K., and Jing Lyman. *Report of the National Strategy Session on Women's Self-Employment.* Washington, D.C.: Corporation for Enterprise Development, 1986.

Greenbaum Susan D. "Economics and Ethnogenesis in 19th Century America: A Comparison of African American and Euro-American Mutual Aid Societies." Manuscript on file, Dept. of Anthropology, University of South Florida, 1991.

Hammond, Dorothy, and Alta Jablow. *Women In Cultures of the World*. California: Cummings Publishing Co., 1976.

Hoke, Linda. "Creating An Entrepreneurial Culture: Microenterprise in the Southern Economy." *Southern Growth* (1990): 1-29.

Joekes, Susan. *Women in the World Economy*. New York: Oxford University Press, 1987.

Katz, Michael. *The Undeserving Poor*. New York: Pantheon Books, 1989.

Kirzner, I. M. *Competition and Entrepreneurship*. Chicago: University of Chicago Press, 1973.

Knight, F. H. *Risk, Uncertainty and Profit*. Chicago: University of Chicago Press, 1921.

LaSota, Marcia, ed. *Women and Business Ownership: A Bibliography*. Minnesota, Minnesota Scholarly Press, Inc., 1985.

Leibenstein, H. *General X-efficiency Theory and Economic Development*. New York: University Press, 1978.

Lees, John. *Committee Systems of the United States Congress*. New York: Humanitarian Press, 1967.

Long, J. E. "The Income Tax and Self-Employment." *National Tax Journal* 35 (1982): 31-42.

MacKinnon, Catherine. "Feminism, Marxism, Method and the State: Toward Feminist Jurisprudence." *Signs* 8 (1983): 635-658.

Mann, Charles, Merilee Grindle, and Parker Shipton. "Understanding Small and Micro-Entrepreneurs." In *Seeking Solutions: Framework and Cases for Small Enterprise Development Programs,* edited by Mann, Grindle and Shipton, 9-30. Connecticut: Kumarian, 1989.

Maryland Dept. of Human Resources. "Business Owners Start-Up Services of Maryland: Program Narrative." Proposal on file, Business Owners Start-Up Services, Baltimore, Maryland: 1990.

Mezzera, Jaime. "Excess, Labor Supply and the Urban Informal Sector: An Analytical Framework." In *Women's Ventures: Assistance to the Informal Sector in Latin America,* edited by Marguerite Berger and Mayra Buvinic, 45-64. Connecticut: Kumarian Press, Inc., 1989.

Michon, Louis. "Women Who are Changing the World." *Development* (1987).

Moore, Henrietta. *Feminism and Anthropology.* Minneapolis: University of Minnesota Press, 1988.

Mott Foundation. "Enterprise Development Programs for the Disadvantaged: Small Steps Toward Big Dreams." U.S. House of Representatives, Washington, D.C., 1989. Mimeographed.

Omvedt, Gail. "On the Participant Study of Women's Movements: Methodological Definitional and Action Considerations." In *The Politics of Anthropology,* edited by Gerrit Huizer and Bruce Mannheim, 373-393. Paris: Mouton Publishers, 1979.

Ortner, Sherry. "Theory in Anthropology Since the Sixties." *Comparative Studies in Society and History* 26 (1984): 126-166.

Pease, Katherine. "Senate Select Committees." Master's thesis, University of South Florida, 1987.

Peattie, Lisa. "An Idea in Good Currency and How it Grew: The Informal Sector." *World Development* 15 (1987): 851-860.

Phillips, Paul and Erin Phillips. *Women and Work: Inequality in the Labour Market.* Toronto: Lorimer, 1983.

Phillips, Ronald L. "Microbusiness Development." Report on file, from Coastal Enterprises, Inc. to the United States Senate Small Business Committee, 1990.

Pivens, Frances Fox and Richard A. Cloward. *Poor People's Movements.* New York: Vintage Books, 1977.

Pivens, Frances Fox and Richard Cloward. *The New Class War.* New York: Pantheon, 1982.

Portes, Alejandro and Manuel Castells. "World Underneath: The Origins, Dynamics, and Effects of the Informal Economy." In *The Informal Economy: Studies in Advanced and Less Developed Countries,* edited by Portes, Castells, and Benton, 11-37. Baltimore: The Johns Hopkins University Press, 1989.

Raspberry, William. "Turning Welfare Recipients Into Entrepreneurs," *The Washington Post,* 28 June 1991.

Reichmann, Rebecca. "Women's Participation in Two PVO Credit Programs for Microenterprise: Cases from the Dominican Republic and Peru." In *Women's Ventures: Assistance to the Informal Sector in Latin America,* edited by Marguerite Berger and Mayra Buvinic, 132-160. Connecticut: Kumarian Press, Inc. 1989.

Saddler, Jeanne. "Small SBA Loans Planned to Put the Poor in Business," *The Wall Street Journal,* 14 December 1990.

Sanday, Peggy Reeves. Introduction to *Anthropology and the Public Interest.* New York: Academic Press, 1976.

Schumpeter, J. A. *The Theory of Economic Development.* Cambridge: Harvard University Press, 1934.

Solomon, Burt. "Power to the People?" *National Journal* (1991): 204-209.

Steinmetz, Ann McCormack. "Doing." In *Doing Qualitative Research: Circles Within Circles,* edited by Margot Ely, Margaret Anzul, Teri Friedman, Diane Garner, and Ann McCormack Steinmetz, 41-105. London: Falmer Press, 1991.

Stevenson, Lois. "Women and Economic Development: A Focus on Entrepreneurship." *Journal of Development Planning* (1988): 113-126.

U.S. House. *Select Committee on Hunger Progress Report.* 98th Cong., 2nd sess., 1984. H. Doc. 98-1176.

U.S. House Select Committee on Hunger and Committee on Banking, Finance, and Urban Affairs. *Hearing on Microenterprise Credit,* 99th Cong., 2nd sess., 1986.

U.S. House. *Select Committee on Hunger Report on Access and Availability of Credit to the Poor in Developing Countries and the United States.* 100th Cong., 1st sess., 1987.

U.S. House Committee on Small Business. *Hearings on New Economic Realities: The Role of Women Entrepreneurs,* 100th Cong., 2nd sess., 1988a.

U.S. House. *Select Committee on Hunger Progress Report.* 100th Cong., 2nd sess., 1988b. H. Doc. 100-1107.

U.S. House. *Select Committee on Hunger Report on Strategies for Expanding the Special Supplemental Food Program for Women, Infants, and Children (WIC) Participation: A Survey of WIC Directors.* 100th Cong., 2nd sess., 1988c.

U.S. House. *Select Committee on Hunger Report on Self-Help Programs: Innovative Options for Achieving Self-Sufficiency.* 100th Cong., 2nd sess., 1988d.

U.S. House. *Select Committee on Hunger Progress Report.* 101st Cong., 2nd sess., 1990. H. Doc. 101-1002.

U.S. House. Select Committee on Hunger. *Hearing on New Strategies for Alleviating: Building Hope by Building Assets,* 102nd Cong., 1st sess., 1991a. H. Doc. 102-14.

U.S. House Select Committee on Hunger. *Hearing on New Perspectives on Urban Poverty and Microeconomic Development,* 102nd Cong., 1st sess., 1991b. H. Doc. 102-9.

U.S. House Committee on the Budget and the Select Committee on Hunger. *Joint Hearing on Microenterprise Development Strategies for Rural America,* 102nd Cong., 1st sess., 1991c.

U.S. House. *Freedom From Want Act.* 102nd Cong., 1st sess., H.R. 2258. 1991d.

U.S. House. "100 Members Cosponsor Hunger Legislation: Key Amendments Included in Education and Labor Bills." News Release, Select Committee On Hunger, 30 July 1991e.

U.S. House. *Select Committee on Hunger 'Hunger' Report.* 102nd Cong., 2nd sess., 1992.

Velez-Ibanez, Carlos. *Bonds of Mutual Trust: The Cultural Systems of Rotating Credit Associations Among Urban Mexicans and Chicanos.* New Jersey: Rutgers University Press, 1983.

Wandner, Stephen A. and Jon C. Messenger. "The Self-Employment Experience in the United States: U.S. Department of Labor Demonstration Projects in Washington and Massachusetts." Report submitted to the Organization for Economic Cooperation and Development Evaluation Panel Number 11, 1990.

Wignaraja, Ponna. *Women, Poverty and Resources.* New Delhi: Sage Publications.

Index

For Product Safety Concerns and Information please contact our EU
representative GPSR@taylorandfrancis.com
Taylor & Francis Verlag GmbH, Kaufingerstraße 24, 80331 München, Germany

www.ingramcontent.com/pod-product-compliance
Lightning Source LLC
Chambersburg PA
CBHW050527270326
41926CB00015B/3113